LOOSING THE CHAINS

LOOSING THE CHAINS:

Religion as opium and liberation

J. Andrew Kirk

Hodder & Stoughton
LONDON SYDNEY AUCKLAND

Unless otherwise stated Scripture quotations are taken from the HOLY BIBLE, NEW INTERNATIONAL VERSION, copyright © 1973, 1978, 1984 by the International Bible Society. Used by permission.

British Library Cataloguing in Publication Data.
A Catalogue record for this book is available from the British Library.

ISBN 0–340–54618–2

Published by Hodder and Stoughton, a division of Hodder and Stoughton Ltd, Mill Road, Dunton Green, Sevenoaks, Kent TN13 2YA. Editorial Office: 47 Bedford Square, London WC1B 3DP.

Phototypeset by Intype, London

Printed in Great Britain by Clays Ltd, St Ives plc.

Contents

Foreword

In a recent paper Dr Harold Turner has helpfully distinguished between three levels at which the Christian mission may operate. At level 1 it is addressed to the individual, calling for the conversion of heart and mind. At level 2 it is addressed to the structures of public life, calling for the righting of wrong and the liberation of the oppressed. At level 3 it is addressed to the 'root paradigms', the unquestioned assumptions which operate (usually far below the level of conscious thought) in both personal and public behaviour. Contemporary Christianity is harassed by disputes between the advocates of levels 1 and 2 – usually bearing banners marked 'Evangelical' and 'Ecumenical' respectively. Level 3 is more uncomfortable, and this is the level at which Andrew Kirk is operating.

Perhaps it is his long residence in a Spanish culture which enables him to attack so many sacred bulls with such panache. His book could be described as an example of what St Paul calls 'taking every thought into captivity to Christ'. One of his main concerns is to separate the fact of Christ from the whole world of what our culture calls 'religion', and to distinguish the liberating action of Christ from what can often be the enslaving embrace of religion. That 'religion' is the name for a species which embraces the Christian gospel is one of the assumptions which he calls into question. But his sharpest and most effective thrusts are against the most pervasive assumption of them all, namely that truth is unknowable and that since there is nothing to hear from beyond ourselves, we can spend our time on the 'inner journey', listening to ourselves.

Third level mission is uncomfortable. It is the really radical mission. Oddly enough, the word 'radical' is usually applied to theologians as a term of praise when they question or discard elements of Christian belief on the basis of the contemporary assumptions of modernity. The genuine radical is the one who is prepared to question the reigning assumptions on the ground of the gospel. Of course, if truth is unknowable, there can be an endless exercise of 'dialogue', with the understanding that no one will in the end be proved to be right or wrong. But what matters is that we should lay hold of the truth. This is the passion of this book.

Andrew Kirk's book surveys a very broad range of both 'religious' and 'secular' elements on the world scene. Inevitably those who are specialists in one or other of these fields will have questions to ask. But it is very important to listen to those who are the 'generalists', and especially to those who, like the author, have had a living encounter and engagement with both world religions and secular ideologies in several parts of the world. The book is about bondage and liberation. I think the attentive reader will find it a genuinely liberating word.

Lesslie Newbigin

Preface

Many people who have read widely on the subject and who have had long contact with people of different faiths and their literature have explored in depth the entirely fascinating yet immensely complicated world of religion. They have witnessed to the great difficulties they have encountered in bringing some kind of order out of the complexities of religious beliefs and practices which are part of the daily life-experience of thousands upon thousands of communities.

Even more difficult has been the attempt to relate one variety of religious reality to another in a way which makes some kind of mutual understanding possible. To cap it all, the vastly different approaches which Christians make to other people's religious experiences, customs and systems seem to sow confusion, rather than bring light. In a word, religion in all its countless manifestations lays many traps, even for the most careful.

Thus it would seem foolhardy for somebody like myself, who has begun to think seriously about these issues only in the last few years, to venture boldly into such hazardous waters. My excuse, if such is needed, is that the number of concerns out of which I am writing may be, in their combination at least, peculiar to me.

These concerns (inevitably) come from my background and experience. The overriding one has been expressed time and again by people who identify with what is generally known as liberation theology: it is that religious beliefs and practices, in so far as they lend themselves to manipulation, either to legitimate the privileges of the powerful or to rationalise the situation of the disadvantaged, must be denounced and transformed (evangelised).

There are other concerns too, discussed in more detail in the Introduction, such as the failure of many writers in this field to take seriously the gains that have been made in some of the secular criticism of religion, and the seeming lack of care that some show in submitting their assumptions about knowledge and reality to rigorous criticism.

I want to try to raise a few of what seem to me to be rather neglected issues in the present heated discussion within the Christian community about the merit, or otherwise, of other people's faith convictions. It may just be that someone who comes to this task, not having been intensively involved in dialogue with people of different faiths (yet having met many), but caught up with other crucial matters of Christian mission, such as the liberation of the poor, witnessing to a militantly secular culture, involvement in political action and exploration of the meaning of authentic evangelism, may have different perspectives to contribute which also should be heard. Obviously ignorance is no virtue, but neither should 'expertise' be allowed to foreclose the debate.

Two exceedingly generous friends, Lesslie Newbigin and Colin Chapman, whose credentials in the area of the discussion of religions is beyond question, have read through a draft of this book. I am most grateful for their perceptive and helpful comments and suggestions, many of which I have incorporated into the final text. Needless to say, I alone bear responsibility for what has been said or left out.

I want to express my thanks to David Wavre, the former religious books editor of Hodder & Stoughton, for agreeing to publish a manuscript by me in this area. I hope that in some small measure I have repaid his evident courage. My gratitude also goes to James Catford, who, in the face of my great trepidation in actually finalising the manuscript, has shown much patience. He and his staff have worked hard to eliminate some of my errors and iron out a number of the deficiencies. They are to be commended for carrying out a difficult task. If the result contributes in some small way to further the calling of Christians to be agents of Christ's work of liberation in the world, it will have been worth all the apprehensions with which it has come to birth.

Andrew Kirk
Pentecost, 1991

Introduction

For the last twenty-five years or so, the main challenge facing Christian theology across the globe has been to reflect seriously on outstanding social and political issues. In the process the nature, content and method of theology have all come under intense scrutiny.

Responding to the German Marxist Ernst Bloch, Jürgen Moltmann wrote his epoch-making *Theology of Hope* in 1964. This has been followed by something like a dozen more books from the same pen on themes related to the social reality of human community in the modern world, including: *The Crucified God*, *The Church in the Power of the Spirit* and *The Open Church*. Other Continental Europeans addressing the same problems have been Metz, Gollwitzer, Hromadka, Ellul, Lochmann, Käsemann, and in Britain, Preston, Forrester, Elliot, Bauckham and Leech. In the USA, among white theologians writing about political concerns during this time, we find Lehmann, West, Gottwald and others (see Kirk 1980).

It is to Latin America and the black communities in the USA and South Africa that we must look for the most original and provocative contribution to political theology. (Also in the last few years theological reflection, arising out of solidarity with the suffering peoples of Asia (*minjung*), has gathered pace in countries like the Philippines and South Korea.) Since about 1967, liberation theology and black theology have held centre-stage, and in many ways set the agenda for the theological task on all continents. For the first time in some 1500 years creative theological reflection has been taking place outside the Latin, Germanic, Slavic, Hellenic and Anglo-Saxon traditions of Europe. Theology in the 'Third World' has taken its rightful place as a major factor in the Church's consideration of its calling and mission in the contemporary world.

Meanwhile, in Africa, Christians have been seriously engaged in thinking through the meaning for the Church and its witness of the struggle to create a sense of nationhood, following the colonial era; a struggle made doubly harder because of the fierce economic colonialism that has replaced the former political variety. They are also having to respond theologically both to traditional African religious beliefs, values and customs, and to the rapid 'Christianisation' of the continent south of the Sahara, particularly as evidenced in the phenomenon of the independent Churches. Institutional racism in South Africa, Marxist governments in Ethiopia, Mozambique and Angola, and tribal conflicts in some parts have also presented a major challenge to Christian thinking and action.

Contact with Islam – sometimes violent contact (notably in Nigeria and the Sudan) – is also provoking the African Church to reassess its strategies and its theological commitments. The overwhelming fact of major religions with long histories and deep cultural roots also sets the context for the Church in Asia. From the Middle East to Japan, in every nation the Church represents a tiny minority of the populace. Therefore, of necessity, it has had to work out what it believes about the gospel of Jesus Christ in the context of the dominance of other ways of looking at reality and human life. It has found itself confronted by resurgent religions or ideologies, which are often hostile to the Christian faith, strongly opposed to evangelistic work and sometimes looking for a unity between the State and religion which might well threaten the functioning of minority beliefs.

Major religions are, of course, no longer confined geographically to a line east of the Bosphorus and north of the tropical region of Africa. Since the 1950s, mainly because of widespread immigration from Asia, North Africa and Turkey, Islam, Buddhism, Hinduism and Sikhism now have millions of adherents among people who are full citizens of the various nations of Europe. Moreover, for reasons largely connected to the end of the tacit consensus in the West that Christianity was the religion of the culture, many Westerners have turned to the East, seeking for religious compensation in place of an illusory pursuit of happiness through the accumulation of possessions.

Hence the Church in the West, although still conscious of a mandate to witness universally to Jesus Christ, now discovers that Christian faith is not the only option for those trying to break out of a sceptical, secular environment to find meaning beyond the visible world. In Europe, at least, only a small minority hold to a serious belief in the truth as it is in Jesus. A realistic assessment of the situation has, therefore, led the Church in the West to face the fact that significant groups of the population now follow a diversity of religious practices, either as devotees or as very occasional participants.

This new situation has been a major factor contributing to the rekindling among Christians of the debate concerning the relationship between their beliefs and those of people belonging to other faiths. Just as politics and ideologies have proved to be the greatest challenge to theology during the last quarter-century, so religious plurality may well pose the fiercest examination of Christian theology, far into the next millennium.

Encounter with major religions is not, of course, a new event for the Church. In the modern era, at least since the fifteenth century, giants of the Christian faith have been grappling positively with the issue of other beliefs. (And, of course, the early Church, in a different context, also knew the reality of an immense plurality of religious beliefs. Indeed, most of the new converts to Christian faith would have been former members of one religious group or another.)

Missionary pioneers and leaders of the last two centuries have had to struggle through conflicting ideas and approaches to reach their own conclusions. In this century names like Andrews, Stanley Jones, Zwemer and Kraemer stand out, though perhaps only because they are more well-known in the West than Christian leaders from elsewhere like Devanandan, Chenchiah, Chakkarai and Appasamy.

In recent years the number of people who have tried to relate their Christian faith to the world of religions is quite considerable. The growing number of weighty and influential works being written from all sorts of angles demonstrates just how crucial a question is being posed for Christian mission.

The current setting of the challenge for Christian faith by other well-established, self-confident and ascendant religious beliefs almost certainly provides new elements for thought and action. For one thing, the Western theological tradition no longer shapes so dominantly the search for an adequate response; Christians immersed from birth in cultures heavily influenced by Islam, Hinduism and Buddhism are also making their views known from different perspectives. For another, the rapid 'paganisation' of Europe has caused the Church there to lose most of whatever residue of missionary confidence may have survived the shattering blow of two major wars and the threat of nuclear annihilation which, in spite of a considerable lessening of tension between the super-powers, has not yet become a distant past memory. If the gospel has so singularly failed to help create a genuine peace, built on shared values, mutual respect and common policies, what right have Western Christians to export it triumphantly to other parts of the globe?

The rapid decolonisation of Africa and Asia from 1947 onwards has stimulated a rewriting of colonial history considerably less favourable to the Western powers than that formerly portrayed. Moreover, the abject failure of the rich industrial nations (mostly with a Christian tradition) to take relevant steps to halt and reverse the growing gap between the affluent and the destitute worldwide also calls into question the gospel's power to make a substantial impact on the values and actions of Western leaders (some of whom, at least, claim strong Christian convictions).

However, I believe that the growing new fascination with the question of religious pluralism is mostly due to the way the present climate of relativism in Western culture has broadly come to dominate the manner in which theology in the West is facing the challenges of the hour. Under the impact of philosophical positivism, springing from a particular view of the scope of the scientific method, the idea that human beings can actually grasp final truth about the reality of the universe and the human condition is ridiculed. Despite the fact that philosophers maintain that the verification of knowledge is still the prime philosophical question, the claim to be able to know the truth has been scrapped as an anachronistic relic of an extinct age. The only thing we know for certain is that we cannot know anything with any final assurance – to parody Descartes, 'I think, and therefore I do not know who I am.'

This relativistic climate has thoroughly permeated modern theology in certain key areas, most notably, perhaps, in the realm of personal ethics. Now relativism is making its greatest impact in the field of religious life and thought. John Hick's so-called Copernican revolution (Hick 1977:120–32) is perhaps the clearest manifestation of an attitude which finds it intolerable to consider even the possibility that some religious beliefs may be absolutely valid while others may be mistaken, or even deluded (see also pp. 53–58, 95–97, 163–165 and 171–173, below). Certain fundamental Christian concepts like humility and concern for the worth of others are brought into play to demonstrate that absolute claims over against other beliefs should have no place in Christian thinking and practice. Such claims are often defined as 'fundamentalist', and then, naturally, it is easy to dismiss them.

However, the climate of relativism has only conditioned

modern theological thought in a patchy fashion. So, for example, theologians who are thoroughly tolerant of the legitimacy of most religious beliefs will, at the same time, remain intransigent about racism, feminist concerns and human rights (to name a few major issues). Those who may criticise a high view of the Bible's authority will nevertheless appeal fervently to selected verses and passages if these seem to support particular beliefs they happen to hold.

Such apparent inconsistencies should not cause surprise. They are the inevitable outcome of the fatal flaw built into the notion of relativistic belief: it eliminates itself by its own arguments. Hence, relativism can never be a solid basis for approaching the fundamental questions of life. In practice it has to be constantly qualified, or even refuted by those who feel most drawn to it emotionally and existentially. Without an implicit, unexpressed appeal to the notion of truth, every statement would have to be so qualified that human discourse would be impossible.

It is in the area of an authentically Christian approach to truth, which is related to questions about right human action, motivation and transformation, that I see the way ahead for a global Christian theological interchange concerning the claims and reality of religions today. As will become evident, I believe that some of the conclusions which some expressions of political theology have, in general, drawn concerning the humanly alienating power of religious life help to bring a hitherto neglected perspective to theological reflection on religion in the modern world.

Perhaps the overriding concern of theology in the interfaith debate of recent years has been the authenticity of the experience of God which either people of non-Christian faiths claim for themselves, or which some Christians claim for them. Considerable attention has also been focused on the salvific potential of other religions. As is well known, in the interests of simplifying the diverse approaches which Christians have taken to major religions, a typology of responses has been suggested.

One tradition has been called *exclusivist*. Basically it

claims that the one true God, known through the Hebrew and Christian scriptures, has taken the initiative to create the only way by which human beings may be reconciled to him, thus ending an inherent enmity. That way is through the historical figure of Jesus Christ, who had to die to enable people to be forgiven and cleansed of their guilt. No other possibility of salvation exists.

All religions, as such, are under God's judgement, for they are the result of human beings' tendency to create beliefs and perform certain actions to protect themselves from the disturbing consequences of their separation from God. Thus it is that they seek to find their own path of salvation through piety, good works or elaborate ritual. All such activities, however, are futile, for they ignore the inherently idolatrous nature of human life out of touch with the living God.

Religious commitment, therefore, is not only not a privileged way of encountering God, it may well be (as apparently it was in the case of the Pharisees) the greatest stumbling-block to knowing him truly. The message to people of other faiths is not, therefore, 'Pursue your convictions with greater sincerity and dedication, and you will be rewarded for your great commitment,' but, 'Repent of your religious achievements and receive God's free gift of salvation in Jesus Christ of Nazareth.'

Another tradition has been termed *inclusivist*, for it seeks to make sense of the evidence of God at work within religious faiths other than the Christian. People starting from this position argue that it is manifestly absurd to dismiss all religious commitment as if it provided nothing more than manifold ways of avoiding a true confrontation with God. People of other religious faith undoubtedly have genuine glimpses of the majesty and greatness of God. They also believe that sincere contrition is necessary for those who want to approach him. The doctrine of grace is by no means confined to the Christian faith.

So, as some have put the case, we may not presume to claim we know where God is not. All we *can* say is that

Jesus Christ, as the fullest account God has given of himself, is the norm for discerning God's saving activity in all religions. Every knee shall indeed bow one day before Jesus as Lord, because all will recognise that the noble elements in their faith find their real fulfilment in him.

A third tradition, of more recent vintage, is labelled *pluralist*. In a sense this position, by denying that Jesus Christ is the ultimately relevant fact by which all religious belief is to be judged, tries to cut the Christological Gordian knot. Rather than seeing in Jesus Christ the completeness of God's self-revelation, this view holds that he is unique only in the sense that he is unparalleled among other distinctive manifestations of the divine. Rather than confessing that Jesus Christ is the one Lord over all, this view asserts that the one Lord who has manifested himself in other names is also known as Jesus. Consequently, for this way of looking at faiths, Jesus Christ becomes central only for Christians, while God's salvation is available within any major religious tradition, according to the particular wisdom that has been learned.

This typology, however carefully defined, may not do justice to the subtlety of some people's approach to other religions. Sometimes the three positions are too sharply etched, giving a caricature of what individual people actually believe. Trying to fit diligently constructed opinions into a typological strait-jacket may mean that some really important concerns are not heard.

It is not, however, for this reason that I personally am dissatisfied with much of the present discussion. I agree that all Christians are called to give an account of their faith in Jesus Christ. This will mean deciding, among other things, whether confessing Jesus Christ as Saviour and Lord implies a conflict with the religious beliefs of other people, or whether one looks for points of comparison and integration or whether one treats each religion as a cultural variation of a common conviction, equally applicable and authentic within its own historical development. My disquiet concerns the essentially abstract nature of the debate. It is too often conducted at the level of ideas and ideals, with little or no reference either to concrete expressions of the religions in question, or to the social reality of religious communities in the modern world.

Put another way, so much of contemporary inter-faith dialogue seems to ignore the social and political context and impact of religious convictions. Hardly ever does it seem to acknowledge, for example, the seriousness of the Marxist challenge to the ideological function of religion. Indeed, in many ways the dialogue starts from assumptions more consistent with Hindu or Greek philosophical beliefs than from the bedrock of the Christian view of God as one who cares passionately about liberation from all forms of bondage, about justice, about the defence of the poor and about the community values of the kingdom.

The fundamental religious question for our age is not whether we experience God's reality in some way or another, but whether we are truly liberated from both internal and external alienations in order to be able to pursue his justice, practise his mercy and walk humbly with him. I find it strange, for example, that in spite of great poverty, endless examples of exploitation, violence and corruption and the racist undergirding of caste purity and impurity, Christians in India are still so reluctant to work theologically from the kind of liberationist perspective that has been elaborated in Latin America.

One might make a number of conjectures why this is so. Some might say that Latin American Christians have not had to cope with religious pluralism (not strictly true, incidentally). Others might suggest that the intense Hindu and Buddhist interest in salvation from the deceit of physical desire has permeated Christian consciousness, making it less responsive to the challenge of social transformation. In an Islamic context, perhaps, it is natural for Christians to share the intense disgust that Marxist atheism (identified as one form of Western materialism) evokes among Muslims. Thus, a more dispassionate look at the Marxist systematic and comprehensive social critique of existing societies becomes ideologically and emotionally extremely difficult.

Whatever the case, there seems to me to be a large dimension of the Christian faith which is hardly represented in the inter-faith encounter. Failure to allow the challenge of a complete liberation to affect the agenda of dialogue is leading to a serious diminishing of its scope and creating a sense of unreality about the way in which religious beliefs affect the behaviour of individuals, groups and nations.

The question of both truth and falsehood, and right and wrong, cannot be avoided. Or, to put it another way, every religion in practice devises its own criteria to verify and legitimise its customs and beliefs by appealing to a number of overarching concepts (like solidarity, tradition, stability, rationality, synthesis, enlightenment, and so on). The verification of truth has been, is and always will be the crucial question facing humanity. However, if Christians are to be involved in the discussion it cannot be limited either to the conceptual beliefs of religious traditions and ideologies or to the values which flow from them.

Inter-faith dialogue becomes an anachronistic pursuit unless it is willing to confront the suspicion, arising from the observation of real existence, that religion is often (if not usually) a manifestation of human alienation and a cloak for all kinds of injustice. Here Christians are going to have to decide how they will react to the belief of many in a post-Enlightenment culture that religion is an illusory crutch or a false consciousness which obscures the real causes of suffering and poses false solutions. Will they tend to see in other religions an ally to confront a godless, impoverishing and ultimately destructive creed (humanism in its many forms), or will they face the challenge as part of God's way of purifying faith and action, even if this means sometimes joining dissenters in sharp and categorical denunciation of religious convictions?

The purpose of this book is to begin to relate the highly fruitful, if disturbing, insights coming from the radical tradition of political theology to the current inter-faith debate.

To borrow a phrase of Kenneth Cragg's, it will attempt to do theology in 'cross-reference'. In this case the reference-point will be the dual acid-test of whether religion acts as opium, and is harmful to the user, or whether it acts as a liberating force in every human situation. In this way the perennial phenomenon of religion will be viewed through an alternative grid. I believe it will offer an altogether more realistic framework for assessing theologically the significance of the religious spirit in a rapidly changing world. Perhaps it may contribute something to a deeper consideration by Christians of what God is calling us to do and to be, in and for our generation.

After an account in chapter 1 of some of the contemporary discussion about the nature and function of religion, I move in chapter 2 to the celebrated attack on religion in all its forms made by Marx, Nietzsche and Freud. In chapter 3 I seek to demonstrate that a relativistic and pluralist view of truth is quite impossible, both in theory and practice. Chapter 4 outlines in very broad terms the central convictions of the major religions of the world, with the primary purpose of setting them in the context of the secular challenge to religion. It is not intended to provide even a brief introduction to the full scope of their beliefs. Chapter 5 develops the critique of pluralism, this time in the context of a theory of religions. I begin to explore the thesis that there is something inherently different about the gospel of Jesus Christ in comparison with the focus of religion, and I finish with an account of why those who believe that God was fully revealed in Christ can be confident about truth.

The comparative ease with which, in the course of history, commitment to Jesus Christ has been subverted from its original intention and has become another religious way of life is the subject matter of chapters 6 and 7. In the latter, I also suggest ways in which the community of disciples may so order their life that they can become a more liberating force in society than they usually tend to be. In chapter 8 I look at part of the text of the New Testament to discover how the early Christians related to people and communities who espoused beliefs and practices markedly different from their own. Clearly, this is not a comprehensive survey (that would probably run to several volumes in its own right). Nevertheless, the passage chosen (the second half of the Acts of the Apostles) gives an excellent sample, including as it does some of the key texts in this area.

The final chapter attempts to draw together the many threads of the argument. It stresses again my concern that God's truth, which is revealed, public and therefore available as a means of judging, correcting and transforming all our beliefs and actions, should be applied in all circumstances as a liberating power. I emphasise that the discernment of truth is not a matter of possession and ownership, but of grace and calling. We cannot control it, but we can recognise it genuinely and surely when we are prepared to live according to its requirements, whatever the cost. I also argue that, whether we are a religious believer or not, whatever may be our particular philosophy of life, notwithstanding any desire we may have to uphold a relativistic view of existence, we have no option but to live on the basis that absolute truth and error are final realities in the universe.

Finally, I make – and, I hope, justify – the assertion that the gospel of Jesus Christ is true: firstly because it cannot fit into the 'projection theory' of religion, and secondly because, in its inner integrity, it is wholly resistant to any kind of manipulation in which it can become the means of promoting any other ends than those which spring from its own liberating aims as declared and manifested in the unique life of Jesus, the Messiah.

1

A Never-Ending Story

'Do you believe in a God who can change the course of events on earth?' 'No, just the ordinary one!'
—**from a survey on religious beliefs**

'God is not so much dead as tamed.'
—**LeRoy Moore**

Religious, in spite of statistics

For many years past, it would seem, there has been a fairly steady decline in regular church-going throughout Western Europe. However, accurate figures are hard to come by, suggesting that once again the old saying is true: 'There are lies, damned lies, and statistics.' In any case, though such a decline reflects people's lack of formal commitment to Christian faith, it does not necessarily tell us much about the presence or absence of religious sentiments of one kind or another.

There is considerable evidence, from interviews and general observation, that many people believe in some kind of God, pray from time to time, claim a variety of 'religious' experiences at different points in their lives, and continue to view some religious ceremonies (like baptism) as important to family life.

Hence, some observers maintain that commitment to the beliefs and functions of traditional religious institutions cannot serve as an accurate measure of the depth of religious feeling in the community. For a whole host of reasons the majority of people in our Western societies do not express their beliefs by attending church activities.

It has been suggested that, for fear of losing face or because they find it almost impossible to say exactly what they believe, most people today prefer to keep their religious convictions largely secret. Also, there has been a general overall decline in commitment to specific organisations – not only the churches, but also political parties, trade unions, sports and social clubs, football teams, and so on. This may be due to the amazing choice of leisure-time activities open to the public. It could also reflect a general view within our society that too definite a commitment to any organisation somehow denies freedom.

There can be little question that for most people the life and activities of the churches are seen as part of an alien world. Having no longer grown up within regular earshot of Christian worship and teaching, they find crossing the threshold of the church (both the building and the community) a strange and perhaps even threatening experience. Today, particularly in certain urban areas, the church and what it stands for seem as remote as a trip to Venus.

Doubts about the possibility of openly confessing an orthodox Christian faith have been around for a long time. Many factors have contributed. The old popular view that science has consigned orthodox religious beliefs to the scrap heap of history still persists in many people's minds. Then, in a society where individual freedom to follow one's own inclinations is so highly prized, traditional religion seems to entail a set of beliefs imposed from without and enforced by a variety of not always very subtle sanctions.

Perhaps the most powerful force accelerating the decline of religious practice is the view that it is essentially a leisure activity, and, as such, is but one among many equally valid pursuits. Church-going might therefore be seen as a vaguely desirable pastime, were it not for the fact that life is already filled by so many other necessary events.

It may not be too far fetched to suggest that shopping has in some ways become a 'religious' substitute for worship in church. I am intrigued by the design of a large shopping complex close to my home. It does not require much imagination to see it as the modern equivalent, in a bizarre way, of the medieval cathedral. On the outside it has twin towers in the front and a single tower at the back. Inside it is almost cruciform, with a long 'nave' leading to a large round open space, and steps going up (as if to a high altar) beyond. On either side of the concourse and around the centre circle are the shops (most of them well-known chain stores). The greatest weekly attendance at the serious business ('service') of buying the goods on display begins at about 10 o'clock on Saturday morning.

Can we not see here (and in countless thousands of similar places throughout the Western world) an example of a building constructed to the glory of human enterprise in which people come to marvel at and participate in human ingenuity and production? Quite simply, though most people might want to deny it, in practice the worship of Mammon has taken the place of the service of God. There is a compelling logic, demonstrated in the real world, in Jesus' words, 'Where your treasure is, there your heart will be also.' The novelist Thomas Hardy makes the same point in rather different words: 'the irresistible, universal, automatic tendency to find sweet pleasure somewhere which pervades all life, from the meanest to the highest, had at length mastered Tess' (Hardy 1978:157).

However, whatever effect popular views of science, or the constraint on freedom imposed by religious institutions, or religion as a leisure activity, or the time-consuming nature of shopping may have on the erosion of open religious commitment, that is not the end of the story. Human beings cannot, and therefore do not, live by bread alone. As one person has boldly claimed, basic human religious needs have not changed notably since the late Ice Age (Greely 1973).

Carl Jung says the same, using different words: 'religion is as real as hunger and the fear of death; it is the strongest and most original of all man's activities; although it is the activity which more than even sexuality or social adaptation is thwarted in modern man'.

It has been suggested that one of the major reasons why there appears to be such a discrepancy between what the Christian faith requires and what people calling themselves Christians actually believe, and how they behave, is the strong emphasis in Christianity on correct belief. The argument is that most people are uninterested in creeds and confessions; they want a religion that works to their satisfaction. To say that 'not God, but life, a larger, richer, more satisfying life, is, in the last analysis, the end of religion' (Schneider 1970) may seem unduly cynical. And yet, in an age used to acquiring all sorts of things because they function, it would not be surprising for many to view God, perhaps unconsciously, in a similar way. An Ethiopian proverb states with great realism that the 'one who recovers from sickness forgets about God'.

The existence of religious experiences, semi-formed religious convictions and occasional religious practices can take a bewildering variety of forms in our kind of society. Bookshops, even in culturally sophisticated towns like Oxford, may have as much on the occult and witchcraft as on all the major religions put together. There is a marked tendency among well-educated people in public life towards belief in some kind of nature cult (as was brought out, for example, in a March 1989 survey in the *Sydney Morning Herald Supplement*). This may be due in part to a welcome concern for the environment, caused by a growing horror at human beings' seemingly inexhaustible capacity to destroy their surroundings, and in part to the popular yet erroneous belief that somehow the command in Genesis (and, by extension, the Christian faith) to subdue the earth is the major cause of our present ecological crisis.

Will religion please stand up!

The trouble with trying to define religion is that it is almost impossible not to be arbitrary. One writer has curtly commented, 'with painful regularity the essence of religion turns out to be what the scholar himself believes' (Hughes 1984). Leszek Kolakowski has said there is a similar problem with art, society, culture, history and politics (Kolakowski 1982:9). However, some of us might be bold enough to attempt a definition of these latter, and yet would shrink from the task of making coherent sense of everything that has ever gone by the name of religion.

There is a real tension between too tight a definition, which excludes what most people understand to be religious feelings and values they are more or less familiar with, and one so loose that it would be impossible not to be religious, however much one protested one's atheism and human-centred convictions. It seems to me that the type of definition which includes as religious anything that any person or group of people holds to be 'sacred', or which inspires devotion or even self-sacrifice, is self-defeating. Such a broad reference, by making almost anything into religion (dedication to creating a beautiful garden, or mountaineering, for example), concludes that, in a sense, nothing is religion.

I am not even sure that one should necessarily include a set of beliefs that inspires moral action. Thousands of people have been highly motivated to work hard, in spite of adverse circumstances, to increase the freedoms and human rights of marginalised peoples on the grounds that thereby they are helping to bring forward the workers' revolution. But these same people would consider the popular religious beliefs and practices of the masses as harmful to the process of their becoming genuinely free.

Another problematical area is the cultural enslavement of religion. By this I mean the unconscious absorption of religious practices into the accepted customs and practices of a given community. Religious rites may be conscientiously followed, but in a way so lacking in conscious reflection on the significance of what is being done that they become simply a ritualised part of ordinary, daily life. Is it then valid to refer to such actions as religious, simply because symbols that could have deeply religious meaning in other circumstances are being used?

Perhaps, instead of trying to nail down a neat definition of religion, it would be better to talk about the essential component parts. An Indian writer has suggested that, at the very least, religion must have a *message* which is received from beyond oneself, an *experience* related to the message, some kind of *community* expression, and a *lifestyle* which seeks to put the message into practice. This attempt at an explanation has the merit of including as a religion beliefs and practices which (as in the case of Theravada Buddhism) do not hold to the reality of a God beyond our sense perceptions.

Even here, however, it is difficult to be consistent. We might well want to include, as religious, convictions which are only vaguely articulated. Yet beliefs coming from beyond ourselves may not have their origin in anything usually thought of as transcendent, but rather in common ideas transmitted within a community (as in the case of particular superstitions – in Argentina, for example, it is *Tuesday*, not Friday the thirteenth one has to be wary of).

Experiences (often of some kind of benevolent presence) may be very real to those who have them, and yet be so personal and so unrelated to anything others claim as to be almost impossible to communicate. Can anything so individual and private be called religious? The community aspect may be almost entirely lacking, for many people apparently do not need to share their convictions about an unseen reality of some kind with others on a regular basis. It has been pointed out that even a religion so well-established as Hinduism lacks a genuinely corporate dimension.

Thus it seems easy to chip away at most aspects of what are normally seen as genuine religious beliefs, leaving little of substance. Nevertheless, we cannot so easily dismiss the fact that on occasions many people seek strength, consolation and meaning beyond their own limited resources. Probably only a few in any society would make coping with the tensions and conflicts of life, using abilities derived totally from within themselves or others, a matter of conviction. There remains a reservoir of attitudes, beliefs and practices among large segments of populations reckoned to be indifferent to conventional religion which have a frame of reference beyond normal human experience. It is these that constitute what is often referred to as 'folk-religion' (numerous other names are given to more or less the same phenomena, such as 'common', 'popular', 'invisible', 'surrogate', 'customary', 'residual', 'implicit', 'diffused' and 'primal' religion).

Popular religious views

Unlike an orthodox catechism, it is difficult to discover a coherent set of beliefs which forms the basic popular convictions of those who, while not adhering to the central doctrines or practices of the major religions, nevertheless perform certain religious rites, either privately or, less commonly, in public. The problem is that it is the outside observer (often someone with more orthodox beliefs) who wants to classify popular religious views and impose upon them some kind of order. The motivation may be simply to try to understand fellow human beings better; or it may have an evangelistic intention – the desire to understand barriers and bridges to the gospel in the popular imagination. There is a danger, therefore, of finding too neat a pattern of beliefs being expressed. Nevertheless, it is remarkable how consistent a picture emerges from research done not only in the Western world, but across the globe (South America, Turkey, India, Japan, to give a few instances). From this it seems fair to conclude that some central beliefs are characteristic of popular expressions of religion everywhere, while at the same time recognising that there are numerous varieties of fringe beliefs which differ according to the place where people live.

Generally speaking, we can say that popular religious beliefs arise from the desire to make sense of the most fundamental questions posed by being alive – birth and death, stages of human sexual development (puberty, courtship, betrothal and marriage), human differences like gender, race and economic inequality, social status, sickness and suffering, success and failure, work, and the reason for existence. They also, perhaps more obviously, afford a way of coping successfully with everyday events.

According to Robert Towler (1974), common religion is marked by at least the following elements: the practice of the rites of passage (in particular some form of 'naming' ceremony); belief in the power of fate ('Whatever will be will be,' 'If my number is on it . . . '); a strong sense of the place of luck in life; a tentative belief in paranormal occurrences (ghosts, the influence of the stars, fortune-telling), and a concept of merit (the balance between moral behaviour and success or failure in life).

In a Christianised context, birth is marked by baptism (usually referred to as 'christening'). There may be a number of reasons why some parents (or grandparents), though non-attenders at church services, persist so strongly in having the baby 'done'. For example, John Habgood, the Archbishop of York, sees baptism as a means of satisfying the immediate need to give significance to the birth of the child or to preserve family tradition (Habgood 1983). The strong pull of continuity with the past has been noticed by others. Towler (1974) sees rites of passage in general as serving to mark a new status for the initiate within the whole community. Baptism, in particular, proclaims that the newly born now belongs to a society which, however vaguely, professes itself to be Christian rather than something else. Perhaps by some kind of intuition 'dedication', when performed as an alternative to baptism, is seen as still leaving the baby 'outside'.

Clearly there is also present an undercurrent of superstitious or 'magic' belief. Baptism not only confers an outward status, but ensures in some way the presence of God, who will keep the child from harm and grant him or her at least some measure of success. Michael Hornsby-Smith (1986) speaks about popular Catholic customs as almost magical insurance policies, employed to guarantee salvation. Towler (1974) relates magical beliefs to people's need to confront any threat to safety or livelihood, in the face of which they otherwise feel powerless. Magic, which is the ritual manipulation of objects, words and gestures in the interests of avoiding bad luck and ensuring well-being, is therefore a kind of 'ritualised optimism' that is designed to end frustration.

Magic seems to be based on a set of reasonably clear assumptions: life is governed by chance; the universe as such is impersonal, and as far as human life is concerned is fairly irrational; certain events bring either good or bad luck (walking under ladders, seeing black cats, magpies, and so on). Good fortune depends upon pleasing an unseen world. It is important, therefore, through mediums or other religious experts, fortune-telling or horoscopes, to discover what is going on 'over there'. The feelings of 'that which controls our destiny' are unpredictable: we can never be certain which of our actions has brought upon us misfortune or suffering. Harmony with the beyond is maintained, or restored, through observing the right rituals (the avoiding of taboos, the use of charms and mascots, incantations, heeding omens, actions associated with the relics or shrines of 'holy' people, pilgrimages, acts of penance, etc.).

So the purpose of magic is to ensure happiness, interpreted as health, financial prosperity and good relationships, and to avoid a breakdown of these things. Underlying the whole process is the notion that evil should be identified fundamentally with harm which comes upon us or our family in an unpredictable fashion.

Though it is said that the idea of merit is particularly strong in the English psyche, it is in fact a common element in all types of popular religion. It takes two main forms.

Firstly, there is the strong notion that suffering is the result of some bad act or attitude committed by the individual or community ('Why has this come upon me?' 'What have we done?'). Therefore, to try to make sense of some desperate tragedy, like the death of a young child in a motoring accident, people will cast around for something to blame. The normal human response seems to be to increase a sense of guilt (in themselves or someone else deemed to be responsible). Conversely, many believe that what they regard as a decently lived life should be rewarded by happiness. Secondly, there appears to be an equally strong notion that eternal bliss in an after-life also depends on the way I behave 'down' here. Again, people often judge their 'chances' on the basis of harm done to others – 'I have led a good life; I have not knowingly done anyone any harm.' For some, merit also extends in the opposite direction: what they have been able to store up while on earth in terms of the harm they have suffered should be recompensed by a safe passage to heaven.

Activities which might be said to have some kind of fringe religious element (such as pop art, folk rock, drug experimentation, sexual mysticism, therapies of all kinds, meditational practices and the pursuit of health) are often connected to a search for personal significance, identity and fulfilment, or perhaps less prosaically simply serve as a substitute for the banality of life. They are attempts to inject some mystery into a routinised life.

Orrin Klapp (1969) says that all kinds of cults are booming in our modern society because identity problems are booming. In Britain, to give one current example, numbers of people are hoping to hear some word of revelation from a mystical past. In a revolt against the excessive obsession with knowledge, they are hoping to gain understanding from the wisdom of the ancients whose commitments led them to build sacred sites like Stonehenge, Avebury, Glastonbury and Silbury Hill.

Klapp says that anybody 'converted' within one or another of the innumerable contemporary cults will experience an enormous emotional release, gain a radically new point of view, share in a common community, and sense that through their new discovery of the truth they are 'arriving home'. Observation of the cults also suggests that a high degree of disillusionment sets in, sooner rather than later, once the gap between promise and fulfilment is discerned.

All these extraordinarily diverse manifestations of popular religion, whether they exalt ancient cultic rites or are expressed in the latest attempt to reach an ultimate experience of ecstasy, seem to relate fairly directly to ancient folk-religion – what Luckmann (1970) calls the indigenous form of a natural religion. LeRoy Moore (1971) predicts that

> the announcement of the death of God (the terminal stage in the process of secularisation) may well be the prelude to a new naming of the divine. A resacralisation which conforms to scientific cosmology will be profoundly this-worldly and may entail a vision of reality surprisingly congruous with or at least compatible to the traditional religions of the American Indian, the African, and the Oriental.

This prophecy seems to find a remarkable fulfilment in what has come to be known as 'New Age Philosophy'. Though notoriously difficult to define under clear and concise headings, nevertheless 'New Age' thinking groups together a number of characteristic themes, concerns and convictions. Philip Seddon (1990) believes that in one sense

> the New Age is *all the new movements*: particle physics, the Human Potential Movement, alternative medicine, fantasy art, vegetarianism, animal rights, peace, astral journeying. More, it is the cross-fertilization of ideas between movements that lends coherence, for instance the line that moves from conservation to ecology to spirituality to paganism.

At the end of a section looking at the historical antecedents to the modern 'New Age' phenomena, Seddon concludes first of all with a quotation from the *Independent*

Weekend magazine (30 September 1989): 'the new culture is the consummation of all previous cultures, for only the combined energy of our entire cultural history is equal to the new quantum-leap of evolution', and then with his own comment that in this culture 'Indian, Egyptian, Greek, Aztec and Mayan mythologies are re-born' (Seddon 1990:8).

There can be little doubt, and its advocates would not want to dispute this, that 'New Age' ideas are a contemporary manifestation, sometimes in the clothes of certain current scientific hypotheses, of a persistent belief in the health-giving properties of a return to the order of nature and its timeless rhythms:

> at the mythological end of the spectrum, 'Planet Earth' is the Mother Goddess, the great life-giver, the dormant Power who is waiting for us all to be reconciled to *her* so that, attuned to her energies and rhythms, she will release her powers to lead us to the goal of evolution: reconciliation between humanity and her. (Seddon 1990:11)

Common religion and a secular society

Where does all this leave the passionate debate about the status of religion in our technologically orientated societies? If it is true that 'the rumour of God' has been gradually dwindling over many years past, it seems probable that it is the supernatural variety which is in decline; the 'ordinary' one, in its many guises, is still flourishing. Of course, our societies have seen colossal changes over the last two centuries. These have clearly affected the status of religion within the community.

Whatever beliefs still flourish, the orthodox, personal God who saves all who turn to him from their sin and becomes their friend and constant companion on the way has become very remote for most people. As we have seen, a sense of fate has replaced the orthodox belief in God's overruling providence in all affairs. Religion, in any of its forms, has almost entirely lost its overarching social significance. It has little or no influence over the large corporate structures of modern societies: government, business, labour, the military, health and education. At least in subjecting large areas of life (usually considered the important ones) to rational decision-making, humans demonstrate their conviction that it is possible to perfect the world. In this connection it is interesting to note how optimistic both politicians of the traditional parties and the business community are about the ability to solve the current ecological crisis. For them, in contrast to the committed Green lobby, it is a matter of the readjustment of production, rather than of a complete revolution in present patterns of consumption.

According to Mary Douglas (1973;1990), secular societies are organised around ego-centred networks, rather than bonded groups. Among other things this means that the old religious institutions are being replaced by new ones. What the churches are perceived to offer is not what today's generation is looking for. As Sally Moore and Barbara Myerhoff (1977) maintain, people today are looking more for ceremonies and celebration, less for ritual. Religious organisations have flourished in the past on the continuous performance of sacred rites and on the handing down of the correctly defined tradition. Today people want variety. They will exercise their inalienable right of choice. If the commodity does not appear to function for them, they will go for a more 'up-to-date' model, or possibly wait until the 'right' model comes on the market. Many could be said to be playing a waiting game with regard to religion, hedging their bets.

Concerning the presence of religion within the whole civic life of a nation (often called civil religion), there seems to be a considerable divergence of belief and practice between Europe on the one hand and the USA and modern societies like Japan, South Korea and Singapore on the other. In the minds of many people, not least politicians, there is a considerable amount of confusion and inconsistency about the role of religion in relationship to the State. The presence of religion seems to be welcomed as long as it reinforces the corporate identity of a nation in a way which does not upset cherished political rhetoric. Robert Bellah (1969), in his celebrated essay 'Civil Religion in America', says that 'national morality cannot prevail in exclusion of religious principle'. Religion (in the case of the USA this is certainly not Christianity, but some deistic or unitarian concept of God) is given the function of cementing the moral fibre of the community, providing the legitimation of its structures of authority (as in the State opening of Parliament in the UK and the inauguration of the President in the USA) and a sanction for the current ideas about law and order.

In recent years civil religion has fastened on to the vastly overworked theme of the exodus in order to explain and convince doubters about one or another version of the nation's 'manifest destiny'. Certain groups in countries as apparently dissimilar as the USA, South Africa and Israel have invoked the exodus story to uphold their calling to be a 'light to the nations', with the right to dispossess indigenous peoples of their land in order to found a new social order. Manifest destiny has many colours: it can manifest itself in the exporting of 'pure' communism from Cuba to Latin America or Africa, or technological superiority from Japan to South East Asia.

In all these ways religion is deemed by 'the Establishment' – defined by Henry Fairlie as a 'small group of men who use their contacts and influence to put a stop to things they disapprove of, to promote the reliable and preserve the status quo' – to be a useful undertaking. When, however, religion becomes a prophetic voice of protest against the flagrant injustices and corruption of the public realm (whether of government, business or even of the religious establishment), it is told most emphatically to limit itself to pursuing spiritual ideals. Indeed, one can only conclude that the admonition to 'keep out of politics' means basically, 'Speak soothing words about "my" politics and reserve your condemnations for the politics of my adversary.'

Conclusion

Looking at the complexities of religion in Western societies, one is struck by the stark paradox of a declining Church and a rising tide of popular religious expressions of every hue. Rightly or wrongly, Christianity has been judged as too uniform and lifeless, its ideals too perfectionist and uncompromising. As Grace Davie says, to the working class in particular (but no doubt more generally today among a self-indulgent population) being a Christian seems a daunting task.

Our generation wants religious diversity, light entertainment, and not too much long-term commitment. The popularity of popular religion is based on its assumed ability to meet the pressing problems of everyday life, its lack of well-defined doctrines, its decentralised nature, its tolerance of human fallibility, and in some cases on authority figures who wield some kind of mystical power. The God of orthodoxy is seen as a kind of divine schoolteacher who is forever trying to discipline a recalcitrant third form, while popular religion tends to be indulgent – for 'children will be children'.

Religion has survived the long steady drip of scepticism and ridicule because it is felt to fulfil deeply experienced unmet needs. Bel Mooney is quoted as saying (Clifton 1986:36):

> there is a sense of the numinous – of a mystery that hovers at the perimeter of our comprehension . . . It is that sense, and the conviction that there is more to us than getting or spending, that takes me (and my doubt) into the village Church, to keep silent during the creed, yet to admit by my presence the power of old stones, old faith.

Religion – any will do, so long as it seems to operate efficiently – provides the answer to a whole host of demands felt to be part of being human. It gives us a meaning to life, a means of achieving emotional stability, a community to identify with, inner resources to cope with demanding public lives, professionals to comfort us in times of tragedy and stress, a reason not to fear death, a justification for family life, and a way of handling our strong sexual drives. In times of adversity it may fulfil the negative function of providing a scapegoat for ills suffered, or an object against which to rebel.

By and large societies, in so far as they are modern, are not interested in such apparently esoteric questions as whether religious convictions are true or not, or in what ways their claims may be judged authentic. No doubt this is the major reason why so many appear to be so gullible, prepared to put their trust in phoney religious quacks and their spurious medicines. What is immediately important is to provide a solution to one of a number of problems. It may be too much of an exaggeration to say with James Leuba that 'so long as men can *use* their God, they care very little who he is, or even whether he is at all' (James 1960:483); nevertheless, there is much evidence that people want their religion tailor-made. We might rephrase the exultant cry of the people of Babel in the plain in Shinar as, 'Come, let us build ourselves a religion.'

Though originally written over a century ago, the following quotation magnificently illustrates the perennial inclination to regard religion as an instrument for gaining benefits in this life and the one to come: 'Men who have tried it [prayer] have confidently declared that there is no sleeping partner in any business who can begin to compare with the Almighty' (May 1949:51). It is hardly surprising that some in our culture have reacted strongly against every form of religion, depicting it as the cause of emotional, mental and social diseases, not their remedy. To these polemical crusades against religion, in whatever dress it parades itself, we now turn.

2

Stealing Fire from the Gods

'If there is a God, atheism must strike him as less of an insult than religion.'
—**Jules de Goncourt, *Journal***

'There is no social evil, no form of injustice whether of the feudal or the capitalist order, which has not been sanctified in some way or other by religious sentiment and thereby rendered more impervious to change.'
—**Reinhold Niebuhr, *Christian Realism and Political Problems***

'God is dead, Marx is dead, and I am not feeling too well myself.'
—**Andre Glucksmann, quoted in *Time* magazine – 5 September 1977**

The acknowledged masters of religious derision

Not only does a firm religious commitment seem to be, for most people, gradually withering away and dying out through confusion, uncertainty, substitute interests and indifference, but its demise has also been actively promoted by some of the most important philosophers, scientists, social analysts and writers of the last century and a half.

One could mention a veritable galaxy, or some might

prefer 'rogues gallery', of famous people who have sought to discredit and remove out of harm's way any reference to religion as a vital constituent of human life. At the top of most people's list would come three intellectual giants of the middle and late nineteenth century and the early twentieth century: Karl Marx (1818–83), Friedrich Nietzsche (1844–1900) and Sigmund Freud (1856–1939). Each one, in a very different way, grew up in a family deeply affected by religious beliefs and duties, but nevertheless developed ideas profoundly hostile to any kind of religious view of the world.

However, at the end of the twentieth century it might seem strange, if not slightly absurd, to use these three champions of militant atheism as models of the modern anti-religious spirit. Partly because governments based on Marxist thought have failed to produce a society genuinely free from want, greed and exploitation, in which a spirit of sharing and co-operation pervades all levels of life, and partly because Marxist theory is seen to lead inevitably to the suppression of freedom, Marx is no longer considered a reliable guide to the way human communities will or should develop. More and more he is seen as an interesting historical figure, whose ideas could only be meaningful had history not taken a very different path from the one he predicted.

Justifiably or not – and the debate will probably never be concluded – Nietzsche's extravagant ideas about good and evil, the will to power, the superman and the eternal return have been largely discredited because of their association with the rise of Nazi and Fascist philosophies and policies in the second and third decades of this century. A general revulsion against the total substitution of the moral tradition of Europe implied in Nietzsche's thought and its consequences for personal ethics and the conduct of political power leaves him as an unattractive prophet of a new type of humanity for the future. Moreover, the pathetic end of his own life – twelve years of total withdrawal from the real world, helplessly dependent on the care of his mother and sister – seems to belie his own rejection of weakness and all that is close to death.

The creator, father and stern defender of psychoanalysis, Freud, is also the subject of much disillusion today. Though there are still some working in the field of mental health and illness who accept and work with his theories of the unconscious and repression, many more now consider them either too weak on empirical evidence or too narrowly conceived to be any longer a convincing guide for understanding both normal and abnormal behaviour. Long ago renowned colleagues like Jung and Adler decisively broke away from Freud's psychoanalytical assumptions.

In the light of a generalised scepticism about the value of the ideas of these three people concerning human social life and consciousness, one might well ask, Why bother about them? The answer, I think, is relatively simple: they embody in their thinking a cultural mood which, though perhaps not quite so self-consciously today, still dominates the intellectual atmosphere that most children begin to breathe from their first day at school onwards. J. P. Stern in his book on Nietzsche underlines the abiding influence of their views:

> Friedrich Nietzsche belongs among those very few thinkers – Karl Marx and Sigmund Freud are the others – whose standing as modern masters is undoubted: had they not lived the life of modern Europe would be different . . . All three are part of our nineteenth-century inheritance – our inheritance from an age which, more than any other, believed in ideas, and in change, reform and revolution through the power of ideas. (Stern 1978:13)

Though it is true that a number of the details of their ideas have been strongly criticised and reassessed, many of their general assumptions about human life (not least about religion) are still taken for granted. Therefore, those who continue to believe that human existence without firm religious convictions is severely impoverished and stunted should be willing to listen to the major representatives of the contrary view. People who are religiously committed often seem to be in danger of underestimating the force of the critique of religion in our contemporary secular world. They may employ one of a number of defence mechanisms to avoid facing the painful reality that they now represent a small minority in a Western world usually apathetic, but sometimes vigorously hostile, to any dimension of life beyond the sensual.

The discovery of implicit religion may be one such ploy: by this means we can comfort ourselves that almost all that most human beings do has some kind of religious significance. Religion becomes extremely elastic, as ill-defined as the proverbial length of a piece of string. Thus we avoid the conclusion that either deliberately or by default most of our neighbours have rejected what we think is the most important reality of life. Another strategy, used most frequently by people of Asian origin, but also by others, is to link the decline of religious belief and practice with a generally decadent, if not wholly moribund, culture in the West. In this way it is easy to ignore the substance of the secular criticism of religion and to avoid having to admit that in part that criticism is absolutely right and wholesome.

In my experience many of those who are heavily involved in building bridges of friendship and understanding between people of different faiths tend to ignore the kind of criticism which secular thinkers like Marx, Nietzsche and Freud aim at the place which religious beliefs and institutions have occupied in human communities. It is natural and easy to suggest that all religious people of good will ought together to seek ways of combating the effects of a godless culture and promoting a Godward consciousness.

It is profoundly mistaken even to give the impression that people of different religious traditions are necessarily on the same side in the struggle to reverse the all-pervading embrace of secularism. The truth is, I want to argue, that many of those traditions genuinely stand condemned. Therefore, for the sake of the real in our relationship to

God, we need to listen attentively to what is right in the secular view of the world.

For these reasons it seems apt that we should attempt to feel something of the force of the break with religion of our 'three musketeers'. Therefore I will attempt to allow each of the three in turn to put their point of view on religion, before offering a personal assessment of what seems to be valid in their respective critiques. At a later stage in the book, we will discuss the limitations and inadequate assumptions on which they seek to build an alternative world.

Flowers on the chains

At the age of twenty-five Marx wrote a letter (September 1843) to one of his first collaborators, Arnold Ruge. With absolute seriousness he sets forth the burning conviction which became his life's work (Marx 1972:8): 'We realise all the more clearly what we have to accomplish in the present – I am speaking of a *ruthless criticism of everything existing*.'

Later in the same letter Marx states that criticism must be directed first and foremost against religion and politics, for between them they represent human beings' basic concerns. Religion, he argues, mirrors their theoretical struggles and politics their practical ones (11).

Marx begins his public career, as it were, with a radical critique of religion, stating that 'the criticism of religion is the premise of all criticism'. In his opinion, it is both the extreme expression and fundamental cause of a false human consciousness, because it gives both the wrong account of and the wrong solution to our pressing experience of misery: 'the criticism of religion is, therefore, *the embryonic criticism of this vale of tears* of which religion is the halo' (12).

In his forceful criticism of the place of religion in the life of human beings and societies, Marx could use a powerful turn of phrase. Without knowing any other sentence from the vast volume of material which he wrote in his lifetime, most people can quote the famous aphorism that religion 'is the *opium* of the people'. In the same passage Marx also refers eloquently to religion as 'the sigh of the oppressed creature, the sentiment of a heartless world, and the soul of soulless conditions' (12).

By opium Marx meant that religion acts in human affairs as both a deadener of pain and as a tranquillising drug. It helps to make human beings insensitive to their real needs and problems, encouraging them to escape into an unreal world from the pain of an inhuman and unfree existence. He goes on in the same context to state forcefully why he objects so strongly to religion: 'the basis of irreligious criticism is this: *man makes religion*; religion does not make man . . . Man is *the human world*, the state, society. This state, this society, produce religion, which is an *inverted world consciousness*, because they are an *inverted world*' (11).

The criticism has three main parts to it. First, the object of religion, God, is a *projection* of human beings' failure to solve their own problems. Marx undoubtedly took over the basis of his criticism from the philosopher Ludwig Feuerbach. This latter desired, once and for all, to do away with any reference to another, ideal world which somehow became the controlling factor in human life. For human beings to become wholly free it would be necessary to put the study of humanity in the place of the study of God (anthropology instead of theology). In his celebrated book *The Essence of Christianity*, Feuerbach summarises his belief in the following way:

> He who says no more of me than that I am an atheist, says and knows nothing of me. The question as to the existence or non-existence of God, the opposition between theism and atheism, belongs to the sixteenth and seventeenth centuries, but not to the nineteenth. I deny God. But that means for me that I deny the negation of man. In place of the illusory, fantastic, heavenly position of man, which in actual life necessarily leads to the degradation of man, I substitute the tangible, actual, and consequently also the political and social position of mankind.

> The question concerning the existence or non-existence of God is for me nothing but the question concerning the existence or non-existence of man. (quoted in Lichtheim 1961:17)

For Feuerbach, and even more for Marx, religion presents a picture of an upside-down world, or one seen in reverse, as in a mirror. People who insist on interpreting life in terms of beliefs and values drawn from religious traditions are like those who would try to drive a car with their eyes fixed on the rear-view mirror. The real world ahead can only be taken in by looking away from what lies behind. Religious thinking creates God as an all-embracing, benign compensation and refuge for our feelings of loss and helplessness. He is part of the problem of not being able to see the world *as it really is*. He obscures the vision.

Second, religion is a factor of *alienation*. In practice it has functioned to weaken human beings' resolve to change their situation of misery and oppression. In the real world religion has become a powerful tool in the hands of the dominant class (all those who control the way society works in their own interests) to explain and legitimise the way things are. Religion has been and continues to be used by those who exercise political and economic power as a foundation for justifying situations of gross inequality and for resisting any major attempt to bring about a much fairer system.

It is interesting that, for all his devastating criticism of religion, Marx does actually acknowledge that in some sense it is a protest against suffering. In its portrayal of a heavenly realm of perfect love and compassion for others, in which violence, pain and grief will be no more, it passes a powerful negative judgement on this world. Unfortunately, however, the element of protest has usually been effectively neutralised by doctrines which suggest either that the world is so evil that any attempt to change it will only make matters worse, or even worse, that it is destined to deteriorate more and more until God rescues the righteous out of it by a cataclysmic intervention. For example, it is easy for those expert in the art of distortion to demonstrate that the revolutionary programmes for changing the present economic system that are proposed by the godless Marxists are but one more demonstration of the deterioration.

The third plank in Marx's critique treats religion as an *illusion*. Though religion attempts to give some kind of explanation for suffering as a result of 'man's inhumanity to man', it always gives the wrong one. In Marx's thought the fundamental reason why human beings are 'everywhere in chains' is because either willingly or by force they have bartered away their humanity for the sake of some kind of economic gain. While a system remains in operation which forces human beings to sell themselves in the market-place for the sake of gaining bread and perhaps a few pieces of cake, they will never discover their real humanity as free, creative, expressive beings. Under the present economic system, increasing the amount of capital has become the chief end of the productive process. As a result human beings have become subservient to, rather than genuinely masters of, their economic life.

Marx might have summed up the real problem of human existence in the world by saying that man has been created for the sake of production, not production for the sake of man. He did, in fact, use a more elaborate and technical language about the fetishism of commodities, but the meaning is much the same: human beings collectively have created and defend a system which trivialises and corrupts their true potential.

Part of the reason for Marx's virulent dismissal of religion lies in his overpowering conviction that the whole travail of history could come to an end only when human beings (particularly the working classes) fully understand *the true nature* of the problem of their exploitation, of which capitalism is the latest (and destined to be the last) manifestation. So, the chief problem with religion is that it expresses a false picture of what is wrong with human society. It diverts attention away from the real causes and, to use Marx's language, envelops the world in a mist of confusion. A final quotation from the young man of twenty-five should clarify the entire thrust of his rejection of the religious spirit in human beings: 'The abolition of religion as the *illusory* happiness of men, is a demand for their *real* happiness. The call to abandon their illusions about their condition is a *call to abandon a condition which requires illusions*.'

Marx's criticisms of religion are not only accepted by those who follow his thinking on other matters, they have become a common stock-in-trade for all kinds of people who believe that religious beliefs and practices belong to an age in which humanity is struggling to break free from childhood to become a mature adult in the world. Their extraordinary power to convince people to abandon religion, and even actively to counteract its influence, is due mainly to the highly attractive view that at last the real nature of the way the human mind and society works has been exposed. In other words, they claim to be part of a strictly 'scientific' account of how we human beings behave. Conversely, all defence of the religious dimension of life has to be understood as a smokescreen and conspiracy to defraud the vulnerable and ignorant.

The death and burial of God

The first major work that Nietzsche wrote was called *The Birth of Tragedy*, about the creation of Greek tragic drama. His own personal life was in many ways one of deep tragedy, loss and contradiction. Born the son of a Lutheran pastor, he came to oppose vehemently the whole Christian faith and its system of ethical values. Preacher of the virtues of strength and the affirmation of physical life, despiser of weakness, sickness and failure, he had to resign, when only thirty-five, from the chair of classical philology at Basel University on health grounds. Four years later, after a catastrophic rupture from his closest friends Lou Salome and Paul Ree, he began to write, in utter dejection and solitude, his most famous work, *Thus Spoke Zarathustra*. His last twelve years were spent in complete mental withdrawal and loss of all human contact.

Whether Nietzsche's trenchant views on the decadence of Western culture – due in his opinion to the reactionary influence of Christianity – were a contributing factor to his mental illness we will never be sure. One of his closest friends, Overbeck, believed that they were. Writing shortly after Nietzsche's death, he says:

> To me it seems quite possible . . . that he did not bring madness into life with him, but that it was a product of his way of life . . . I could not entirely resist the thought that Nietzsche's illness was simulated – an impression derived from my long-standing experience of his habit of taking on many different masks. (Stern 1978:39)

Speaking about the desire of Marx, Nietzsche and Freud to liberate humanity from the illusoriness of belief in God, by fostering as its alternative various forms of self-reliance and self-assertion, Stern adds the significant comment, 'only Nietzsche shows an awareness of the full significance of the loss of religious belief in our experience' (Stern 1978:14).

In his thought, at least, Nietzsche was quite ruthlessly consistent in his virulent dismissal of all belief in God. He believed that he, among others, was the herald of a totally different consciousness for the world, one in which any reference to God would literally be a thing of the past, 'the greatest recent event – that "God is dead", that belief in the Christian God has become unbelievable – is already beginning to cast its first shadow over Europe' (Nietzsche 1977:343).

The Christian faith in particular stood like a gigantic stumbling-stone in the way of a new kind of society struggling to be born. Its vision of what is good and what is evil is the exact opposite of the values which must be extolled by the human race of tomorrow. According to Stern, 'the denigration of man's life on earth and the subordination of man to God are Nietzsche's two principal objections to Christianity' (Stern 1978:97–8).

If human beings are to become strong, noble, masters of their own destiny, then they will have to reject Christianity root and branch: 'The Christian faith is from the beginning a sacrifice: the sacrifice of all freedom, all pride, all self-confidence of the spirit, at the same time enslavement and self-mockery, self-mutilation . . . ' (Nietzsche 1977:46). According to Nietzsche, religion and philosophy, throughout the period of Western civilisation dominated by the Christian faith, have been used as powerful weapons by the resentful, envious and afraid to deny a full experience and enjoyment of life to those valiant enough to break free from all moral restraint.

Nietzsche's view is a total contradiction of Jesus' teaching in the Beatitudes, 'Blessed are the poor in spirit . . . Blessed are the meek . . . Blessed are the peacemakers' (Mt. 5:3, 5, 9):

> The ultimate indictment of Christian belief . . . is that it does not recognise man as the master of the universe, since it insists that freedom, authority and knowledge, vouchsafed to men, are all relative to an alien, outside decree, and rendered intolerable because they are derivative . . . Man cannot reach the highest enhancement of his powers until he has destroyed in himself his belief in the divine. (Stern 1978:96–7)

Nietzsche's life-work was to set forth the conditions for the birth of the superman (*Ubermensch*). This was a collective name for certain ideals and a way of life, 'in him the cardinal vices of lust, lust for power and egoism are transformed into positive values' (Stern 1978:103). Nietzsche speaks of the coming into being of a 'higher age', 'a more manly, warlike age . . . which will above all, bring valour again into honour! . . . An age that will carry heroism into knowledge and wage war for the sake of ideas and their consequences' (Nietzsche 1977:283). This new age would be an advance. It would be the rebirth of civilisation, in which a 'stronger species of man' would create its 'own new tables of values'.

In order to describe the kind of new species which he envisages, Nietzsche turns to certain, carefully chosen 'heroes' of the past:

> then there arise those marvellously incomprehensible and unfathomable men, those enigmatic men predestined for victory and the seduction of others, the fairest example of which are Alcibiades and Caesar (to whom I should like to add that *first* European agreeable to my taste, the Hohenstaufen, Friedrich II), and among artists perhaps Leonardo da Vinci. (Nietzsche 1977:200)

But he retains his greatest praise for Goethe, and in doing so provides the closest profile of the superman that we can find anywhere in his writings:

> Goethe – a grand attempt to overcome the eighteenth century through a return to nature, through a going-*up* to the naturalness of the Renaissance. He bore within him its strongest instincts: sentimentality, nature-idolatry, the anti-historical, the idealistic, the unreal and revolutionary. Goethe conceived of a strong, highly cultured human being, skilled in all physical accomplishments, who, keeping himself in check and having reverence for himself, dares to allow himself the whole compass and wealth of naturalness . . . a man to whom nothing is forbidden, except it be *weakness* . . . A spirit thus emancipated stands in the midst of the universe with a joyful and trusting fatalism, in the *faith* that only what is separate and individual may be rejected . . . But such a faith is the highest of all possible faiths: I have baptised it with the name *Dionysus*. (Nietzsche 1977:49)

As Stern (1978:96) says, 'Nietzsche has no fear of hubris.' Indeed he exalts it and revels in it. It is the beginning and necessary condition for real human freedom in which one wills to overcome the corrupting mediocrity of normal existence, whatever the cost:

> What is freedom? That one has the will to self-

> responsibility . . . That one has become more indifferent to hardship, toil, privation, even to life. That one is ready to sacrifice men to one's cause, oneself not excepted. Freedom means that the manly instincts that delight in war and victory have gained mastery over the other instincts . . . The man who has become free . . . spurns the contemptible sort of well-being dreamed of by shopkeepers, Christians, cows, women, Englishmen and other democrats . . . (Nietzsche 1977:38)

The whole philosophy is summed up in one supreme, heroic act of defiance: 'Once you said "God" when you gazed upon distant seas; but now I have taught you to say "superman"' (Nietzsche 1977: 242).

Infantile helplessness

All of our three religious iconoclasts turned to Greek mythology to express their beliefs and desires. For Marx it was Prometheus, who had the audacity to defy the gods in order to further the knowledge of human beings. For Nietzsche it was Dionysus, the symbol of boundless vitality, fecundity and lack of all restraint. For Freud it was Oedipus, who in a series of tragic encounters killed his father, married his mother and eventually put out his own eyes.

Freud closely linked the origin of the religious impulse in human beings to his supposed discovery of the 'Oedipus complex':

> In a study of the beginnings of human religion and morality which I published in 1913 under the title of *Totem and Taboo* I put forward a suggestion that mankind as a whole may have acquired its sense of guilt, the ultimate source of religion and morality, at the beginning of its history, in connection with the Oedipus complex. (Freud 1973:375)

The Oedipus complex in the thinking of Freud is the repressed guilt associated with the shameful and unacknowledged desire of the male child to eliminate the rivalry of the father and to have sexual relations with the mother. Freud reckoned to have discovered a whole layer of unconscious motivations in the patients he treated for emotional disorders. In his quest for the underlying cause of neurosis he put forward the theory of the libido, an energetic subterranean sexual drive, as the chief explanation.

Neuroses manifest themselves in human beings in the form of a substantial divorce between the concrete reality of the world and the imagination of the person. So, a neurotic may act in a way wholly inappropriate to his or her age: a fully grown adult will behave as if he or she were still a small child. Individuals may regress to an earlier stage of human development because they cannot handle the conflict engendered by their failure to redirect their libido:

> To obtain neurosis one must assume that the individual forbids himself, or part of his personality forbids him, fulfilment at the very point in its development to which the libido has regressed. If this happens libidinal impulses find expression only in symptoms and thus the neurosis is formed . . . Symptoms and neuroses are pathological expressions of certain wishes or impulses, the expression being pathological if wishes or impulses are and remain unconscious. (Wollheim 1971:140, 151)

Freud came to believe that all religious sentiments were manifestations of guilt and neurosis. God is a human creation whose function is to assuage the sense of suppressed outrage which the child directs against itself when it realises the enormity of its own sexual fantasies. The need to believe in God represents a regression to an immature state of human development: 'the ultimate basis of man's need for religion is infantile helplessness'. It is a childish hangover which must be abandoned if a person is to become a psychologically integrated person.

Religion is the result of a terribly obsessive illusion, whose driving force is wish-fulfilment. As such, for Freud, it is destructive of emotionally normal behaviour:

> Common man cannot imagine Providence otherwise than in the figure of an enormously exalted father. Only such a being can understand the need of the children of men and be softened by their prayers and be placated by the signs of their remorse. The whole thing is so patently infantile, so foreign to reality, that to anyone with a friendly attitude to humanity it is painful to think that the great majority of mortals will never be able to rise above this view of life. (Isbister 1985:213)

So, religion can be seen as the projection of a set of deep-seated, conflicting desires, an inadequate response to the basic need to resolve conflict. Its effect is to compound the problem. Freud believed that he had uncovered the secret of the origin of religion as a universal phenomenon among all people. He thought that there is a close parallel between what is early historically or in the life of the species and what is early psychologically in the life of the individual:

> the events of human history, interactions between human nature, cultural development and the precipitates of primeval experiences (the most prominent example of which is religion) are no more than a reflection of the dynamic conflicts between the ego, the id and the super ego . . . repeated upon a wider stage. (Isbister 1985:219)

Freud believed that he had discovered in his clinical work, particularly in his analysis and explanation of dreams, an overarching theory to account for the highly persistent and, in his view, deeply irrational place of religion in most people's lives. Like Marx and Nietzsche, he viewed religion as the major obstacle to humanity discovering the real cause of its distress and embarking upon the conquest of a new and more glorious stage of human development:

> The meaning of the evolution of civilisation is no longer obscure to us. It must present the struggle between Eros and Death, between the instinct of life and the instinct of destruction, as it works itself out in the human species. This is what all life essentially consists of, and the evolu-

> tion of civilisation may therefore simply be described as the struggle for life of the human species. And it is this battle of the giants that our nurse-maids try to appease with their lullaby about Heaven. (Wollheim 1971:232)

What can we say?

Those whom we have chosen to represent the critique of religion did not mince their words. It would be difficult to harbour any illusions about the wholly negative judgement they pronounced upon religion and all its works. They openly professed atheism, and saw their calling as an appeal to humanity to abandon its illusions and build a brave new world without God and the futile consolation of religious convictions and practices.

Though they would probably not have used the word of themselves, the hidden influence of their religious background suggests that it would not be inappropriate to call them 'prophets'. In a different setting, with vastly contrasting motives and purposes, they embarked on the same kind of mission as was entrusted to Jeremiah, 'to uproot and tear down, to destroy and overthrow, to build and to plant' (Jer. 1:10). In a strange sense the prophetic tradition of the Judaeo-Christian faith was a necessary condition for both their critique and their attempt to transform the thinking and consciousness of the human race. Erich Fromm says of Freud, 'under the disguise of a scientific school Freud realised his old dream, to be the Moses who showed the human race the promised land, the conquest of the Id by the Ego, and the way to this conquest' (quoted in Isbister 1985:178).

In another culture, not so strongly influenced by biblical ideals, they might not have been so highly motivated to seek to deliver humanity from what they considered to be its various alienations. Change, the sense of a higher destiny for human beings, and a refusal to accept any kind of accommodation with falsehood are all elements of the prophetic view of things. In spite of their own intense conviction that their methods of analysis and description were strictly scientific – though there is plenty of evidence to suggest that they made of science a fetish – the importance and influence of their massive intellectual work cannot be understood apart from its prophetic power to pronounce both judgement and the coming of a new world. Thus science became in their hands not some kind of dispassionate tool for building and testing theories about the world, but a weapon of war with which to rout enemies and conquer the territory which hitherto the latter had held.

Therefore Christians who take seriously the biblical message should at least be able to understand the reasons for their passion, even if they do not accept many of their conclusions. In fact, Christians, by an exercise of the imagination, should be able to go even further and, having listened carefully, take on board what is absolutely correct in their description of the role which religion often plays in the life of individuals and communities. The cursings of Balaam should be heard, digested and acted upon, and thus turned into blessings (cf. Num. 23:11; 24:10).

To a certain extent this listening and consequent action is happening in some Christian quarters: for example, in the case of Freud, in the attention given to properly researched and understood counselling methods (such as 'Clinical Theology'); and in the case of Marx, to the way in which 'base communities' are combining in their life a joyous celebration of the Christian gospel in worship and evangelism with concrete action to end particular acts of discrimination and violence by wealthy and powerful people against vulnerable sectors of the community.

The Argentine theologian Jose Miguez (1976) argues that there is a profound atheism propounded at the heart of the biblical disclosure of God. Paradoxically this atheism is expressed categorically in the first and second commandments of the decalogue: 'You shall have no other gods before me. You shall not make for yourself an idol . . . ' (Exod. 20:3–4). In the case of Israel, God makes it clear that it is part of his active purpose to overturn all idolatry, and especially the idolatry of religion itself when it is used to sanction injustice, or to harbour illusions about the real world, or to be a means of escape from pain, conflict or the challenge to change situations that cause suffering among vulnerable people. In this sense God demonstrates that he is willing to overturn even his own gifts (temple, sabbath, law, land) in order to save his people from self-deception and self-destruction.

In the Hebrew and early Christian tradition, to know God is to fulfil the terms of the covenant, by relating oneself to 'the God who really is' through the only means that he will accept, the obedience of faith:

> When faith is made into something separated from the whole meaning of that covenant, when it closes in on itself in a religious universe from which man and his need – and specifically, his physical, material need – are excluded, God will not acknowledge any more such 'faith': it will 'profit nothing'. (Miguez 1976:67)

Atheism, in whatever guise it comes, should be a salutary reminder to all who profess that God is central in their lives to consider who it is they honour and what is the appropriate response to his character. Atheism is only possible if theism is a valid way of understanding the meaning and purpose of the universe. But not any theism will do. Atheism becomes an obligation when religion reflects a distorted or manipulated view of God. Frankly, much of what goes by the name of religion today is little more than the religious mirror-image of the consumer-society. Human beings are considered as a consuming species in which religious products (like 'spiritual peace', 'salvation', 'eternal life', 'healing') are announced and promoted like any other good or service. Using a prophetic irony in no way inferior to that of the most brutal opponent of religion, Miguez comments: 'sometimes we seem to be so concerned that man . . . accepts [our] religion as a "standard" product, as a kind of spiritual bath, almost like a brushing of the teeth or a gargle before going to bed'. He then asks the serious question: 'does man really exist in the many stereotyped and impersonal religious activities which we plan, or is what exists simply an organisation and a product whose success we want to guarantee?'

Unless people committed to religious beliefs and activities are able to take seriously the validity of prophetic atheism, they will be endlessly prone to self-delusion about what is right and wrong in life. Religion forever walks on the precipice overhanging the abyss of idolatry. History is a catalogue of the way in which religions and sects have created false images of God and then followed them. Idolatry is the running after gods who are tolerant of injustices and the oppressive use of power, who are more concerned with the stability of society than with its transformation, who promise peace, harmony and prosperity to those concerned only with their own lives or the well-being of their own family or community. All religions are idolatrous, in so far as they become ways, however subtle, of manipulating God or the unseen world for the sake of personal gain, however noble the motives may appear.

Does one exaggerate too much in suggesting that most religion, most of the time, is like flowers adorning the chains, or like resentment against life, or like the infant's need of parental protection from the harsh rigour of the real world? It condemns itself unless it is willing to let go of all false securities, all illusions and all defence mechanisms.

Those who find a strong conflict between commitment to a particular form of religion and the godlessness of our contemporary secular culture are right, in one sense. But in another sense, may not an atheist be closer to the true God than the religious devotee? This is a question that I wish to continue to explore, at the same time demonstrating that all forms of an absolute atheism, most especially those of Marx, Nietzsche and Freud, are also the products and expressions of idolatry, illusion and alienation.

3

Nothing but the Truth?

'In Roman society all religions were to the people equally true, to the philosophers equally false and to the government equally useful.'
—**Edward Gibbon,** ***Decline and Fall of the Roman Empire***

'That which has been believed by everyone, always and everywhere, has every chance of being false.'
—**Paul Valery,** ***Telquel* I**

'Integral to, if not ultimate for, religious life is the question, what is true?'
—**William Cantwell Smith,** ***Christ's Lordship and Religious Pluralism***

Atheists and agnostics

Cultural moods seem to swing giddily from side to side. Committed atheism is generally out of fashion today. The powerful views of our 'three musketeers', Marx, Nietzsche and Freud, resonate only faintly among small groups of intellectuals, some of whom have made a personal pilgrimage from some form of theistic belief to its rejection. Much more acceptable in the present climate of opinion is a vague agnosticism, tinged with indifference. Professor Keith Ward, in his series of BBC radio broadcasts *The Turn of the Tide*, and his book of the same name (1986), gave plenty of evidence to suggest that doubt about the possibility of God was on the wane. It was being replaced by a willingness to consider that belief was at least as plausible as unbelief.

People committed to the necessity of religious faith may take this as an encouraging sign that the populations of the West are on the edge of a return from a one-dimensional, materialist view of life to a new spiritual search. However, there are reasons for caution in interpreting the current situation in this way. In the first place, genuine atheism usually reflects a measure of commitment which, though from a religious point of view it is misguided, is nevertheless authentic and honourable. Agnosticism may be a stopping-place on the road to positive belief and commitment. However, in practice it is more likely to spring from a wholly apathetic lack of curiosity in anything other than the immediate and the material. It is likely to be the knee-jerk reaction of someone suddenly forced to switch their thinking about their job, home-life, car or hair-style to the question of God.

In the second place, atheism acknowledges the importance of absolute realities. Atheists are prepared to state categorically that some things cannot be believed and, furthermore, ought not (absolutely) to be believed. Agnosticism, on the other hand, drinks deeply at the well of relativism. It may well be the response of the lazy or confused, rather than the intellectually vigorous, too much effort being required to sort through the incredible number of religious beliefs on offer. It is partly for this reason that common religious sentiments, as we explored them in chapter 1, are not necessarily incompatible with an overall agnostic stance: we cannot be sure of anything, but just in case there is something (or someone) there beyond our world, we will hedge our bets. The former England cricket captain Mike Gatting expresses this view clearly and poignantly: 'I believe in a bit of everything – God, the supernatural, ghosts, superstitions, UFOs. I like to keep my options open' (Gatting 1989: 67).

Relativism in the air we breathe

Our main concern in this chapter is to explore the nature and consequences of a relativistic outlook on life, and show why it is a fallacy, before making comments about the necessity of truth in every area of human existence. Rather than attempt an overarching definition of relativism as an approach to reality, two quotations which speak for themselves will do the task more forcefully (though being part of dialogues within novels, they do not necessarily represent the opinions of their authors): 'What is moral is what you feel good after, and what is immoral what you feel bad after' (Ernest Hemingway); 'Morality is largely a matter of geography' (Elbert Hubbard).

In the first of these quotations right and wrong are made to depend on the subjective reaction of the individual; in the second, upon the accidental factors of history and custom. Relativism, then, views decisions about the meaning of human life and about behaviour as matters purely of personal choice or of the customs and values of culture. A denial of the possibility of being able to come to know the final truth about the universe becomes a confession of faith.

Relativism is deeply ingrained in the mood of Western culture. It is part of what Lesslie Newbigin (following Peter Berger) calls the contemporary plausibility structure. Thus the claim to know the ultimate truth about existence is ridiculed as an anachronistic relic of an extinct age. To consider that some beliefs are absolutely valid, while others are plainly wrong, is treated as an idea from the ark. It is a hangover from a dogmatic, intolerant age out of which we have developed a much more open, broad-minded and comprehensive view of things as they are.

As with so many features of the culture in which we are totally immersed, we do not seriously scrutinise, let alone criticise, the assumptions on the basis of which we accept the prevalent mood. The relativistic outlook has descended on us like a blanket of fog. Within the resulting restricted horizon left to us we may be satisfied that there is nothing else to see. But we do not even know that our vision is seriously impaired. An attempt to clarify the assumptions may help lift the fog and at least give us the possibility of seeing beyond our immediate surroundings. Whether or not we perceive another reality will depend on whether the removal of the fog shows us the glory of another panorama or causes us to close our eyes.

Truth is beyond our ken

There are perhaps four main reasons why our generation seems to have abandoned so emphatically the notion that there are things which are true (i.e., which correspond perfectly to the whole of reality, whether seen or unseen) at all times and in all places. Firstly, there is a widespread belief that all real knowledge is contained within the world. The only things we can be absolutely certain about are those substantiated by generally recognised principles of verification. Only by a proper method of research, followed by experimentation and testing, can we be certain of facts beyond any reasonable shadow of doubt.

Even then we have to accept that all our knowledge is provisional. By its very nature scientific investigation is based on the work and surmises of fallible human beings working individually or in co-operation with others. The observations they make can never be final, nor their perspectives an ultimate reference-point. Results are always open to new discoveries or new interpretations of what is already known. In other words, we can only talk meaningfully about true facts when they are implicitly open to being challenged by methods which everyone recognises as valid. Nothing beyond the world of the senses can be so authenticated. It has to be a matter of belief or opinion, not a question of fact or real knowledge which compels assent.

Secondly, our understanding of the world is subject to

changing patterns of history. No past historical event (say the giving of the ten commandments on Mount Sinai or the absence of Jesus' body from the tomb where he was buried) can possibly claim to be unique or a privileged reference-point for interpreting the meaning of all subsequent events. In the nature of our historical existence we have to be open to experiencing events in the future which will be more significant than those of the past, or to finding facts which disprove either the historical events themselves or the significance given to them within a particular tradition.

The assumption behind this argument is that truth is linked to an expanding rational knowledge of the universe in which there may always be surprises beyond our limited horizon. We cannot know the truth until the end of the story. It would therefore be fatal for humanity not to be open to the possibility of discovering another way of salvation or another moral code superior to all that have gone before. Linked to this view of the relative nature of historical existence is the Marxist suspicion that claims to truth belong to a particular stage in the development of societies from alienation and bondage to real freedom. They are simply the expressions of the dominant group in society, used now to fortify their privileges, but destined to disappear when these groups cease to exist.

Thirdly, it is a truism to recognise that today, more than ever before, the world is full of diverse cultures. Modern travel, the global communications network, and disciplines like cultural anthropology have shown just how varied a world we live in. One of the effects of this recognition, following Ernst Troeltsch's opinion that all religions are true for their followers (Troeltsch 1990), is to hold that beliefs and values belong harmoniously to the culture out of which they have grown. They are true in so far as they express the respective culture authentically. Thus, for example, it would be appropriate to argue for the rightness of sharia law for all those of Arab stock, the dowry system for people from the Indian subcontinent, and ancestor-worship for the Chinese. All these traditions are integral to the culture.

It is of the essence of relativism to assert that no one is in a position to judge the worthiness, or otherwise, of cultural variables. To make judgements about other people's culture assumes a privileged position of superiority from which one is able to discriminate between positive and negative elements, thus returning to the discredited cultural imperialism of the colonial age.

Fourthly, whatever belief system seems to work for those who hold to it must be valid. On this assumption the concept of truth is pressed into the modern preoccupation with the functional. Convictions about life and death, human relationships and moral decisions are true if they help people cope better with the problems they face.

This view perhaps sums up better than any other the contemporary mind-set of post-technical societies. Truth, like any other commodity, is something to be possessed and made to work for our own predetermined ends. So, for example, it is a common view expressed in many counselling techniques that the supreme end is to get people functioning again in a relatively normal way. Thus a technique is accorded the status of truth if it achieves what we want it to. This common view is the exact reverse of the way in which truth has been understood in previous ages, namely as that which makes claims upon our lives, before which we should submit irrespective of whether it is convenient or not, painful or not, or contradicts our cherished beliefs or not.

A great gulf between facts, beliefs and language?

Underlying these assumptions there are perhaps two main convictions: firstly, that beliefs and moral values have little or nothing to do with the world of facts; and secondly, that because truth is ultimate and universal, it cannot be expressed in the finite terms of ordinary human language. These views may at first sight seem highly plausible. However, to have a more comprehensive perspective we need to look at some of their logical consequences.

The major consequence of the split between what are held to be concrete provable facts (for example, that there is a definite causal link between smoking and lung cancer) and people's moral judgements is a kind of languid anarchy in deciding between right and wrong. This can lead to positions which may immediately strike us as wrong, and yet which on the basis of relativism are quite reasonable. For instance, 'the new right' tends to argue that great discrepancies of wealth between the rich and the poor cannot be blamed on an unjust system (free-market capitalism), because the system itself does not intend that result. The notion of justice, therefore, cannot be related to an analysis of what actually happens in society when certain mechanisms operate. Fact and moral judgement are kept apart.

Or take the common practice of abortion on demand. The only possible criterion which can operate in this context is that of subjective desire: is the baby wanted or not? In the case of foetuses showing some abnormality which would lead to disability outside the womb, some parents would still decide to want the child, while others would not. Either decision is equally valid. It is purely a matter of perception and the individual circumstances of the parents, or more likely those of the mother. There is no universally valid criterion, such as the total inviolability of the living organism due to its relationship to God, by which we can decide between life and death. My perception of my feelings and needs is the ultimate touchstone of what should or should not be done.

Another result of this divide is that, because human beings literally have to believe in something, they will turn to all kinds of creeds as a foundation for meaning and action. In the brave new world of some scientific popularisers, science itself will bring about a revolution in our ethical consciousness. According to Jacques Monod (1971), modern societies have not yet accepted the profounder message of science which is 'the defining of a new and unique source of truth, the demand for a thorough revision of ethical premises, and the necessity of forging a new one' that would be based on 'objective knowledge'. Others, who cannot accept the discredited optimism and hidden agenda of the Monods of this world, turn to more esoteric beliefs, like the 'New Age' philosophies, which are based on a witches' brew of so-called astrological science, neo-pagan naturalism and pantheism.

The second main conviction concerns the limitation of language to express truth adequately. It has been forcibly expressed by Archbishop John Habgood (1983:69) in the phrase, 'to know God is to transcend every representation of God'. At first sight such a statement seems convincing enough. It is based on the premise that what by nature is eternal and infinite cannot be circumscribed by the temporal and ambiguous nature of human discourse. Thus every time we want to say something definite about God we are forced to qualify our statements, because there can be no final correspondence between our use of language and the being and activity of God. On further consideration, however, the statement is illogical, if not absurd. If we can only know God truly by going beyond the language we are bound to use to describe him, then there is no way of knowing that it is God we know. Personal knowing is not possible without being able to articulate truly to oneself in linguistic form what one knows.

Guilty of fraud

This observation about the possibilities of language takes us on to look at the essential fallacies of relativism in all its forms. There are two main objections to relativism, and they are both based on observation of what actually is the case. Whereas relativism is itself a belief system, a theory of what some people would like to be true, its refutation is based on the actual way people behave in everyday life: in a passive sense, they are compelled by the very structure of thought itself to think in terms of opposites; and in an active sense, they appeal in many cases to absolute values.

Relativism is denied both in theory and in practice. Let us try to explain this line of reasoning further.

The fatal flaw, built into every appeal to relativism, is that it is bound to eliminate itself by its own argument. We can only affirm that relativism is true on the basis of a reality which denies it, namely that nothing is absolute except the relativistic principle. In other words, to maintain its viability it has arbitrarily to exclude itself. Yet on what possible grounds can it do this?

Another way of demonstrating the impossibility of relativism is by showing that adherence to it demands an absolute commitment of faith which cannot be warranted by the principle itself. Scepticism about the possibility of knowing final and absolute truth demands a strong commitment to doubt, which has to be justified on the basis of a positive commitment to an alternative statement of faith.

If, however, what claims to be true is doubted on the sole basis of a personal choice not to believe, without appeal to any evidence or authority outside subjective experience, there is still an inner necessity to state on what grounds personal choice has been set up as the final criterion of judgement. There is simply no way round the tacit or implicit appeal to another absolute without making all statements into tautologies. This becomes obvious once one begins to analyse the way in which thinking actually operates.

What we are talking about here is the celebrated – and, not surprisingly in the present relativistic climate, fiercely damned – principle of non-contradiction. This has been condemned as an outdated, culturally determined and restrictive way of reasoning. There may be many reasons why we do not like it and which cause us to get angry when others use it to prove a point. Nevertheless, it is inescapably basic to the way we are bound to think. There is no way we can break free from it without actually using it and thus demonstrating its correctness.

Suppose we were to say that the law of non-contradiction cannot be applied to the major religions in order to show that some of their belief systems are incorrect, because that would imply an imperialistic attitude of superiority, we would thereby be affirming that the statement we had just made is true. By the same token, we would also be affirming that the opposite of this statement, namely that the law of non-contradiction must be applied to all religious beliefs, is false. So in the very process of denying the validity or applicability of the principle one is actually using it and thus affirming that it is true also in this case. The principle is being presupposed in the rejection of the principle.

Two crucial observations follow from this discussion. Firstly, that the principle of non-contradiction is a necessary premise if any discussion on any topic is to have any meaning at all. Secondly, that the principle is emphatically not the creation of a Western way of thinking, which is somehow foisted upon other cultural traditions in order to suppress or marginalise them. The fact that Aristotle was the first to recognise the principle is entirely irrelevant. It is equally binding on all human beings, in so far as there are in practice no alternative options open to our reasoning faculty.

Of course, what is still open to debate is whether any one particular statement does in point of fact contradict another. This, for example, is the case with those Christian beliefs which seem at first sight to be self-contradictory, like the Trinity or the relationship between predestination and free-will. In the first case, for example, Christians have always argued, against Jews, Muslims and Unitarians, that there is an essential difference between saying that the affirmation that God has manifested himself as Father, Son and Holy Spirit contradicts the affirmation that God is one, and saying that if there is one snooker ball on the table then there cannot be three. The second statement is an affirmation of a simple mathematical reality: by definition one and three, as numbers, represent different units. The first, however, is not a contradiction, precisely because one and three, in terms of the Godhead, represent a level of reality beyond the strictly mathematical. So the doctrine of the Trinity does not contravene the principle of non-contradiction, only the way in which it should be applied.

The second fatal flaw in holding to relativism has to do with the way we make judgements and act morally. Often decisions concerning the right and wrong way to act have been linked to a careful consideration of the consequences which will flow from them. No act can be said to be absolutely right or wrong apart from the specific circumstances in which it is carried out. The good or the harm which may flow from our activities are the criteria for deciding what we should do.

Of course, weighing up the probable consequences of our actions is a fundamental part of deciding what action to take. But this cannot be an argument against the need for some kind of ultimate moral court of appeal. If the consequences of our actions are given moral status then there have to be criteria for deciding whether they are beneficial or hurtful, or even for calculating the balance between conflicting goods or evils. Moreover, right and wrong need fleshing out with real content. They are not self-evidently true, as we know when we debate, for example, different concepts of justice.

There are two further ways in which ordinary people demonstrate the inevitability of having to appeal to absolute moral values. The first has to do with our practice of judging other people, whether it be our mother-in-law, the prime minister, or some sporting celebrity. The only way we can approve or disapprove of what they do or think is by an implicit appeal to some norm beyond ourselves, which we hold to be binding on both them and us.

The apostle Paul summed up this reality in a trenchant statement, 'at whatever point you judge the other, you are condemning yourself, because you who pass judgment do the same things' (Rom. 2:1). Jesus' word is in similar vein, 'in the same way as you judge others, you will be judged' (Mt. 7:2). If we really believed that moral actions were basically up to the individual, everyone being free to do what seems best to them, we would cease to make moral judgements about others. In practice, however, we find it quite impossible to be consistently *laissez-faire*.

The second way concerns our appeal to certain moral absolutes as quite beyond discussion. Where, for example, the validity of different religious beliefs and practices is concerned, some theologians strongly object to Christians making any kind of exclusive claim on the grounds that such a position denies humility, concern for others and fairness. However, in arguing like this they have elevated their own interpretation of humility, worth and fairness into absolute values. They may or may not be right to appeal in this way to these particular values. But they cannot argue against uniqueness; all they can do is substitute one kind for another.

In so far as a value is absolute if agreed to by all human beings without exceptions, then the rejection of torture and discrimination on the basis of race must count as beyond question. The indiscriminate destruction of the rain-forests, the sexual abuse of children, and cheating in competitive sport (to suggest further examples) would also, on the same grounds, count as wrong whatever the circumstances. To argue boldly against the tyranny of the absolute may be a pleasant way of spending an evening in a university senior common room, or it may make an interesting question for an exam in moral philosophy; in the reality of the everyday world, however, we are forced to be relatively selective in what we are prepared to be morally indifferent about. There are some absolutes which we do not refuse to acknowledge. This is simply a fact of life, which no amount of cunning theory can gainsay.

Blessed are the pluralism-makers

The whole of this argument has crucial importance for the way we look at the subject of religion in the contemporary world. In particular it affects the way we react to a pluralist world and how we approach the question of knowing truth. Let us, in the light of the arguments about relativism so far, begin to discuss each of these points in turn. The rest of the book will continue the debate from a number of different angles.

An astounding plurality of beliefs and lifestyles is an undeniable reality of social existence today. Os Guinness (1983), in a colourful phrase, calls it the 'Smorgasbord Factor' of modern life. Our societies offer an amazing variety of dishes, any or all of which we can taste at a price. There are a quite incredible variety of beliefs, values, lifestyles and political opinions from which to choose. Someone has calculated that in the UK alone there are some 1,000 different religions, sects, cults, philosophies, paths to enlightenment, meditation techniques and fads of one kind or another. As we will see in the next chapter, it would be quite impossible to practise all of these, and so we are forced to make choices. In doing so we decide, according to our own highly personal criteria, what are the relative merits of each, or indeed whether any of them have any merit at all.

It is perhaps one of the chief characteristics of what we call secular culture that such a variety of viewpoints should be allowed so much freedom. Some are inclined to interpret this as a sign of indifference, the kind of inert attitude of a Gallio who 'showed no concern whatever' (Acts 18:17). I think this is unduly sceptical, and would be inclined to view it as the highly desirable gain of a long process of conflict within Europe, in which religious minorities (principally Jews and Nonconformists) achieved equal status with the rest of the population.

There are several reasons for being glad about and defending the right of people to believe and live according to their own consciences. Discrimination against minority groups on the basis of skin-colour, language, cultural customs, or beliefs and values is often due to a sense of being threatened by the unfamiliar. However, once one appreciates that other people's self-identity is able to broaden and enrich one's own, and once one realises that human beings share more in common than divides them, then the fears may begin to evaporate.

Plurality may produce in some communities a sense of agoraphobia, a fear of the open society in which one is able to choose different values from those of the close-knit group. This could be particularly difficult for immigrant communities coming from rural areas in countries which have never allowed individuals much dissent. However, the various totalitarian, authoritarian or paternalistic alternatives are much less savoury. Though there is much generalised criticism of Western individualism, most people, once they know there is a genuine choice, much prefer it to enforced collectivism.

Plurality is based on the right of the individual to be free from manipulative pressures to conform to the opinions or customs of others. In this sense, it is not merely of pragmatic value, but rather echoes values at the heart of the Christian gospel. Every person is a unique individual with a dignity and value before God that may not be violated by others, whatever their motives. People should under no circumstances be used as means to further the plans, projects, schemes, religious convictions or political ends of others, however noble the cause may seem.

Moreover, they should be free to make mistakes. Authoritarian regimes, whether political or religious, tend to treat people as considerably less than adult (i.e., less than human). The God revealed to us in Jesus Christ allows anyone to choose freely to waste their gifts, deny their family and live in destitution among the swine (cf. Lk. 15:11–24). He does not compel them to stay at home, or follow a prescribed path or submit to his authority out of fear of the consequences; nor should we. The choice to enjoy fellowship with God or follow idols is voluntary. Of course, the choice is not equal in terms of the results which will follow, either blessings or a curse. But this fact reinforces the point: God allows us the integrity to make our own choices and the responsibility to accept whatever may come as a result.

The freedom to pursue a plurality of options in an open society is a hard-won gain for a more genuinely human life, which should not be surrendered in deference to spurious arguments about the inviolable unity of nations, ethnic groups, culture and religious beliefs. However, it does not entail a pluralist theory which believes there are no ultimate distinctions between some beliefs and practices and others (pluralism). As we have already argued, such a position is logically impossible and, in real life, impossible to sustain. More important, perhaps, is the fact that the theory is not necessary in order to protect plurality in practice. Tolerance is not the fruit of a careless or agnostic attitude to truth. Quite the contrary. It has sprung from a passionate devotion to the heart of the Christian faith.

Intent on truth

Our final point concerns the apprehension of truth. This is a very large question, to which we will have to return in due course. For the moment, and by way of summing up the discussion of this chapter, I will make one or two negative points. Beliefs, particularly those associated with religion, are not merely the products of culture. Nor is their validity, as we see it, supremely related to their usefulness in promoting personal integration or social harmony. There is the matter of whether they could be true, irrespective of particular cultural embodiments or whether they may produce peace or conflict.

The question *of* truth cannot be resolved by a general quest *for* truth. To believe that truth is something we can discover, starting from where we are, is wishful thinking. By ourselves we do not know in which direction to look, nor what to look for; nor would we recognise the destination when we arrived. Of course, truth has to be tested by experience and in action, for by its nature it is a comprehensive interpretation of all that is. Nevertheless, as a universal fact, its origin must lie outside us, coming to us from another realm of existence. Though truth can only be recognised by us in ordinary categories, it may well cut across many of the things we take for granted. Hence, we often experience conversion as a new framework for interpreting reality.

In terms of the dialogue between different religious traditions, ultimate truth is not negotiable for the sake of harmonious relations. A much more significant and enduring relationship is built on the struggle to understand and appreciate views which conflict notably with one's own. It is probably true that we understand neither the beliefs of others nor our own tradition until we have faced the pain of deep disagreement. We are called, therefore, to work through feelings of being threatened and of our world disintegrating under the pressure of other people's intellectual and personal challenge, in order to reach a more comprehensive appreciation of why we believe what we do. In the course of the process we may have to change some of our dearest perceptions.

That is why people from all religions must allow the full blast of secular scepticism and suspicion to swirl through their cherished beliefs. That is why genuine atheism (such as is, for example, so powerfully and consistently presented by Marx, Nietzsche and Freud) will have a much more purifying effect on faith than apathetic agnosticism. And, who knows, perhaps atheists are closer to the kingdom than those who are content with vague and superficial beliefs.

4

Religion Among the Nations

'Religion may have been the original cure;
Freud reminds us that it was also the original
disease.'
—**Philip Rieff,** ***Freud: The Mind of the Moralist***

'That which we call the Hindu religion is really
the eternal religion; because it is the universal
religion which embraces all others.'
—**Aurobindo**

'We can no more defy the constraints of New
Testament Christology on behalf of Krishna
than on behalf of Osiris.'
—**Kenneth Cragg,** ***The Christ and the Faiths***

Freedom, democracy and religion

Plurality is, as we have noted, a reality of social existence. As a theory of what ought to be, it becomes a comprehensive belief system (pluralism). Both reality and theory present an enormous challenge to the major faiths of the world. To a certain extent the question of truth can be explored by looking at the way in which each handles in practice and in theory the proximity of all the others.

Whatever a particular religion's past history, its adherents are obliged today to come to terms with neighbours who may have a profoundly different outlook on life from their own. They also have to take account of the strong pressure worldwide for self-determination, meaning liberty for all to choose freely those who will govern on their behalf. It is not long before aspirations for an open, democratic society will affect a person's attitude to the faith in which they were nurtured. With the advent of universal education and the immediate accessibility of information and opinions from all quarters of the globe, religious communities can no longer easily shield people from the conflict of ideas.

Plurality, interpreted as the legally enshrined and enforced freedom to practise any religion or none, may become a far greater threat to the integration of religion, culture and personal meaning than either colonialism or the Western missionary enterprise ever was. How, then, have people of different religious persuasions been coping with this phenomenon of our times?

PEOPLE, LAND AND LAW – JUDAISM

For most of their existence the Jewish people have lived as small minorities in hostile surroundings. Only for the period from Joshua to the last of the kings, from Nehemiah to the Seleucid conquest of Israel, from the Maccabees to Pompey and from 1948 to the present day have they been able to govern themselves in their own land. Even in these relatively short spans of time their political freedom has been precarious. Today, as much as ever before, Jews who live in Israel are insecure. The present situation of 'no war, no peace' does not provide the stability needed for long-term planning and the undisturbed opportunity to build a nation.

In spite of the pressures under which they exist, due to intransigent attitudes on both sides caused by fear and resentment, there is a fair amount of open debate going on within the nation. It is a well-known fact that formal religious observance is low in Israel. Nahum Goldmann quipped that Sadat was mistaken to think that by attacking

Israel on Yom Kippur (in 1973) the Egyptian army would find most Jews in the synagogues; more likely they would have been in their beds. In this sense, the secular belief that religion can be separated from ethnic and national identity has been accepted by many Israeli citizens, though it is also true to say that religion operates on many different levels in that country.

Israel, then, is attempting to operate a Western-style, multi-party democracy. Even Jews who do not believe in either democracy or the state of Israel are taking advantage of the possibility of a small corner of power. The situation of Arab minorities who are citizens of Israel is ambiguous. As in many other parts of the world, whatever the constitution may say the minority believe themselves to be discriminated against. Strong interracial tension is produced not only by the wholly unresolved issue of a homeland for the Palestinians, but also by fears of further, massive immigration of Jews from Russia and of a population explosion among Arab families.

What happens to Israel is of enormous consequence to worldwide Jewry. The majority of Jews have elected not to settle in their own homeland. But it is there, if ever the life of the Jewish community elsewhere were to be made intolerable. So most Jews continue to live in the diaspora, as they have done since the exile to Babylon, even when they could return to the land.

Living among the Gentiles brings a number of other problems, principally that of conformism and assimilation. Is the survival of a people and a culture a worthy end in itself? Should Jews remove themselves from contact with other peoples or remain among them to influence society for good, according to the high principles of ethical Judaism? And there is no mistaking the courageous, faithful witness of some Jews to Torah, when Gentiles all around, refusing to acknowledge God's law any more, have become a law to themselves.

These and many other fundamental questions face Jews who have opted to stay within the highly individualistic, materialist, secular and pluralist societies of the West. Some have all but lost their Jewish identity, either through marriage outside the community or through lack of identification within. Community leaders (like the new Chief Rabbi of Great Britain and the Commonwealth, Jonathan Sachs) are deeply concerned by the drift away.

It may be, as Dow Marmur (1982) says, that Jews on the whole have never properly come to grips with secular culture, either being absorbed by it or irrationally resisting everything it stands for. Extreme orthodoxy, particularly when it seems to need to find a certain identity by wearing eighteenth-century Polish peasant clothes, is symptomatic of a deep sense of insecurity. In one way or another it tries to re-create a past ideal. The Jewish faith, however, has always demanded a vision of the future and a concrete mission to live by. The promise to Abraham that his descendants would be a blessing to the nations cannot easily be ignored or evaded.

So how do Jewish parents answer their children when they ask what it means to be a Jew today and what is the point of the religious observances? Is it sufficient to be one small religious denomination among many others, whether huddled together or apart in an immense sea of credal indifference?

The complex question is further compounded by Judaism's long, painful and acrimonious relationship with the Christian faith. There are many strands to this relationship. During the first century of the common era, mainstream Judaism did not acknowledge that Jesus of Nazareth was the saviour of the world sent by God. For them, as Bishop Kenneth Cragg so graphically puts it (1986:15), Jesus as Messiah is pure romanticism, since the world remains unredeemed and God's kingdom is still absent. There is no room for an interim salvation and a hidden Messiah. Easter was either premature or an illusion.

Christians, on the other hand, affirm boldly that Jesus is the only Messiah that there is going to be. They argue that Jews did not recognise the Messiah, because they already held a predefined, dogmatic picture into which Jesus simply could not fit. The ideal was given priority over the real. As a result the two groups went their separate ways. They soon became two very different and apparently irreconcilable ways of interpreting the history and faith of the Hebrew people. From a Christian perspective, the Jewish people largely decided to go the 'way' of Ezra and Nehemiah, the way of nationalism, the law and the synagogue, renouncing their call to universal mission.

As a result, Judaism has in a sense missed out on history. Refusing to be actors in God's play, the Jews have written their own tragedy – not so much the tragedy of suffering (much of which has been scandalously caused by the Church pretending to be God) as of the failure to find their identity and role in the world. There is a real sense in which one dare not claim to be a 'chosen people' unless one is prepared to take on the enormous responsibility of being 'for others'. However, many Jews have now ceded mission to the Gentiles to the Christian Church, on the understanding that they are not included in that mission. They would argue that the initial divine covenant was with the whole human race and was given through Noah. Additional covenants have subsequently been made with the Gentiles (through Jesus or Muhammad). No one covenant invalidates the others.

For deeply understandable reasons Jews are nervous and fearful about Christian evangelistic activity among their community. Given the past relationship of being the vanquished and oppressed, the object of appalling discrimination and virulent hatred, and given the evangelistic methods sometimes used to bring Jews to believe in Jesus, their dismay is explicable and, in part, justifiable. It is not surprising, then, that they view with distrust that interpretation of religious freedom which maintains that it should include the freedom to convert. Thus, for them, plurality would be acceptable if it meant the right to continue one's own traditions without let or hindrance. It would be much more dubious, however, if it implied a free-market trade in religious convictions.

Some Jews and Christians are working towards establishing a new relationship, based on mutual forbearance. It would need to be based, according to them, on the following convictions: that Christians renounce the legitimacy of mission among Jews; that they also accept the magnitude of the Holocaust as an event which demolished the vainglory of a 'Christianised' civilisation; and that Jews overcome their tendency both to stereotype Gentiles and to find their identity principally as the victims of others' hostility.

PEOPLE, LAND AND SACRED ORDER – HINDUISM

Of all the major world religions Hinduism has the reputation for being the most pluralist. Both in theory and in practice it seems to be able effortlessly to tolerate an enormous divergence of belief and practice. One can believe in an impersonal universe, in which final salvation comes through total absorption into the indefinable unity of all things (*Brahman*). One can also believe in one personal divine creator, Shiva, Vishnu or Narayana, whom one approaches through *Bhakti marga* in humility and faith. (This tradition, has produced remarkably fine devotional literature.) There is also a range of literally countless millions of gods in which to believe. As Jesudoss (1986:137) says, Indians do not find it difficult to switch from one god to another, provided the latter is of more help.

Hindus are therefore perplexed by what they see as the 'Semitic' intolerance and possessiveness about God. Christ is interpreted by Hindus as whatever explains and mediates the relation between this world and the other. They are, further, astounded by Christians' insistence on the pre-eminence of one particular historical event as mediating God's salvation. Finally, they are bemused by Christians' emphasis on right belief rather than experience as the starting-point for exploring the way of spiritual wholeness.

It is quite possible that Hinduism has been misunderstood in the West, including by those deeply attracted to it. The reality of religious life in India may be much more complex than the impression one would gain from reading textbook explanations. The question as to what Hinduism actually encompasses is far from simple. The usual answer, that it includes all religious manifestations in India, and among Indians living abroad, with the exception of Islam, Sikhism, Buddhism, Jainism and Christianity, has been sharply challenged.

The word Hindu itself was first used in an Indian book in the eighth century AD, some fourteen centuries after the writing of the Hindu sacred scriptures. 'The term Hindu had originally a territorial and not a credal significance. It implied residence in a well-defined geographical area' (Radhakrishnan 1957:12). 'The word is clearly derived from Sindhu the old as well as the present Indian name for the Indus. From this Sindhu comes the words Hindu and Hindustani as well as Indus and India' (Nehru 1989:12).

From its original application to people living in a particular place, without any reference to their religious beliefs, it is often taken to mean all people living in a geographical location (namely the nation of India), *including* their religion. In a 1977 Indian Supreme Court ruling (quoted in Raj 1986) Hinduism is defined as follows:

> In principle, Hinduism incorporates all forms of belief and worship without necessitating the selection or elimination of any. The Hindu is inclined to revere the divine in every manifestation, whatever it may be, and is doctrinally tolerant, leaving others – including both Hindus and non-Hindus – whatever creed and worship practices suit them best. A Hindu may embrace a non-Hindu religion without ceasing to be a Hindu. Since the Hindu is disposed to think synthetically and to regard other forms of worship, strange gods, and divergent doctrines as inadequate rather than wrong or objectionable, he tends to believe that the highest powers complement each other for the well-being of the world and mankind. Few religious ideas are considered to be finally irreconcilable.

> The core religion does not even depend on the existence or non-existence of God or on whether there is one God or many. Since religious truth is said to transcend all verbal definition, it is not conceived in dogmatic terms. Hinduism is, then, both a civilisation and a conglomerate of religions, with neither a beginning, a founder nor a central authority, hierarchy, or organisation.

Such a definition, though disingenuous in part, shows the theoretical elasticity of the Hindu outlook. However, according to some, particularly other religious minorities, the tribal peoples and the scheduled castes, such a definition is so broad that it simply makes Hinduism synonymous with 'religion'. This could be accepted merely as the premise of the particular Hindu philosophy if it did not have serious political and social overtones as well. Indian Christians and Muslims, because of political sensitivities over the status of the non-caste peoples, are particularly incensed by the assumption that 'no person who professes a religion different from the Hindu or Sikh religion shall be deemed to be a member of the Scheduled Caste' (Presidential Order, 1950; quoted in Raj 1986).

The effect of the definition and the Order is to include all non-caste peoples (Harijans or Dalits) and tribal peoples within the broad band of Hinduism. One of the effects of this, highlighted by the celebrated conversion in 1981 of the scheduled castes of the village of Meenakshipuram in Tamil Nadu to Islam, is to interpret all conversions of these people and the tribals as conversions from Hinduism. Given communal tensions throughout India, and the fear among the minority religious groups of an orchestrated attempt to Hinduise the whole nation, this is an explosive interpretation of the Hindu faith.

Sunder Raj (1986) finds some thirty-five different ethno-religious groups in India, of which only seven can be described as Hindu in the classical sense. He wants to confine use of the term 'Hindu' to the Aryan Vedic *varnashrama dharma* of antiquity, whose marks are the acceptance of the supremacy and priestly duties of the Brahmans, the authority of the Vedas, the worship of Hindu gods, abstinence from pollution through touch, cremation of the dead, and the prohibition against eating beef.

The debate has, of course, quite a profound effect on one's apprehension of the pluralistic tolerance of Hinduism. It may be that the magnanimity which is part of its own sense of being a higher religion than others is not so evident when put to the test. It certainly has the reputation for being able to neutralise all apparent contradictions and contain within itself what others see as incompatible beliefs. It should, then, be largely indifferent to people changing their religious allegiance, even denying their Hindu identity, since its own belief that they are still Hindus is evidence of a comprehensiveness that demonstrates its superiority as a religion. However, as we have seen, many Hindus deeply resent and actively resist conversions to another faith.

As we probe deeper into some of the most fundamental characteristics of this way of looking at life, we notice a much less clear acceptance of pluralism than the usual image suggests. At the risk of gross over-simplification, I will try to pinpoint the main assumptions and characteristics of the Hindu faith.

Basic to all is the concept of eternal order, summed up in the word *dharma*, meaning religious duty, virtue or right situation. Within the sacred cosmic order everything and everyone has their place:

> To have a family place in a jati (subcaste) by family connection is to have a place in the general scheme of things, to belong in a network of rights and duties, claims and obligations of the society. To have no such place is to have no social being and hence no rights. (Stackhouse 1984:206)

The overarching belief in one sacred and immutable order of things helps to explain the incredible tenacity of the caste system in India. Sanctioned by the *Rig-veda*, it came into being at the time of the Aryan conquest of the northern plains of the subcontinent. As its name, *varna* (colour), testifies, it is linked to the encounter of different racial groups. At the top of the caste hierarchy are the fair-skinned peoples, of whom the highest echelon of all belongs to the Brahmans. The lowest caste (Shudras) were of mixed descent through intermarriage, while the 'black' Dravidian peoples became outcaste.

Many believe that the caste system is of the very essence of Hinduism. V. Devasahayan ('Pollution, Poverty and Powerlessness') believes that caste discrimination is based on two factors: a particular understanding of the way the sacred is said to work, and the dominance of the Brahmans who control the required response to the sacred. The Brahmans administered the village temples, thus capturing the social apex of the feudal pyramid. From there they were able to dictate the pattern of socio-cultural developments.

Their two main religious weapons were the notions of purity and impurity, and *karma*. Sacredness became embedded in the whole social order to the extent that professions came to be considered either more or less pure. Those who were assigned the most menial tasks also came to be considered impure and therefore untouchable.

Karma is the accumulation of a person's actions in past lives. Thus, whatever status they may have now has already been determined for them by previous incarnations. There is a wheel or eternal cycle of fortune (*samsara*) which establishes for a person their place within the entirety of existence. The notion of *karma* is full of a strong sense of retribution and desert. The social consequences, when understood literally, are devastating. Any attempt to change one's lot is to tamper with a universal sacred system. The likely result is disaster for the person and their family.

However, within one's social position there is much one can do to ensure a more beneficial existence the next time round. Through the three main ways of reaching spiritual blessing, *jnana* (knowledge), *karma* (action) and *bhakti* (devotion), it is hoped that one will eventually reach *moksha* or liberation from the cycle of rebirths. It is difficult, therefore, to see how social liberation can be a pressing concern of the Hindu faith, according to its most fundamental beliefs. That Hinduism has in the past two centuries undergone a considerable renaissance and reform is to be credited largely to external forces, of which the impact of the life and teaching of Jesus is probably the most important.

SUFFERING, APPEARANCE AND DETACHMENT – BUDDHISM

Although Buddhism started as a movement which dissented from many aspects of the Hindu faith, it is clearly recognisable as a derivative of it. It holds, for example, to a similar view of the unreality and transitoriness of life.

Like Hinduism, Buddhism may be said to include a wide variety of practices, but in its most pure form it is a highly sophisticated, and some would say very abstract, way of dealing with the universal and perennial problem of suffering. In the last analysis suffering is self-inflicted. It comes from the insistence that the self is the centre of reality. Making experience revolve around a personal ego within each of us keeps us chained to an illusory world. For life, the world, is in a state of ceaseless movement (*anicca*), and there is therefore no permanent state of personal consciousness. To believe that there is, and to crave for its fulfilment, is gross ignorance, and this is the cause of one's suffering.

Buddhist belief is the very opposite of the modern narcissistic craving for self-realisation. This can only bring *dukkha* ('ill-being', the opposite of well-being). The way of release from the endless cycle of suffering is by attaining the total elimination of a self-consciousness that wants to maintain an immovable point of reference and meaning within a universe in constant flux.

If the highest good for humans is to achieve a complete detachment from the vain desires of this world, should not Buddhism be completely indifferent to whatever goes on in the real physical world? Is that not illusory? The pure form of Buddhism may be pictured as the serene Buddha, sitting cross-legged on an exquisitely beautiful lotus flower, which in turn floats above a sea of mud. Neither the mud nor the flower nor the Buddha are real, only the smile. That symbolises the bliss of *nirvana*, the ultimate contentment which comes when all ignorance has been finally eliminated.

Like Advaita Hinduism, non-theistic, non-dualistic Buddhism is strictly speaking inconceivable. The goal of the highest human aspiration transcends all possibility of conceptual thought and description. All mere human categories inevitably distort or falsify such a reality. Hence, it is quite impossible to imagine what bliss might be like. In theory it is achieved once we have finally overcome the false division between the subject and the object, when experience of the changing diversity of life becomes the experience of the one. Logically, this is an impossible attainment, since experience of the unity of all things rules out the individual self-consciousness of the one who would know when that state has been reached. In other words, if the subject–object distinction has been wholly overcome, there is no subject left to experience an object distinct from itself.

Also, if we affirm that *nirvana* (emptyness) is beyond all powers of description, then it is quite impossible to say that all our mental representation of it is bound to be wrong. The most we can say (and, of course, many Buddhist teachers, particularly in the tradition of Zen, have said this) is that we can affirm nothing exists or does not exist. The really courageous conclusion of this philosophy is absolute silence. Even language belongs to the world of appearance and flux. In the nature of the case, there is no objective reference-point.

The response to this criticism follows two different paths. The most rigorous uses the analogy of dreaming. While we are in the midst of a dream, it appears to be the only reality there is. However, when we awake, we realise how the dream actually distorted the real world of sense-perception. There are many things we do in the dream which both morally and physically we would not or could not do in real life. The final moment of transcendence from the many to the one is the equivalent of waking from the dream-world of sense-perception into the real existence of pure-consciousness. We know then that this life is unreal, shadowy, confused.

The problem is, however, that unless someone were to return from this state in order to tell us what it is like, we can know nothing about it. It is pure surmise. But nobody could return, for then they would be retreating from the one to the many, from absolute unity to diversity, in order to be able to communicate to us. We could not understand, for we have not yet overcome the barriers of our defective way of thinking. It is interesting to note, in this connection, that one of the main differences between Theravada and Mahayana Buddhism is the *bodhisattva* ideal: the individual who rejects the possibility of release from the painful cycle of rebirths into this life 'and instead throws himself back time and time again into the raging sea of Samsara in order to help others' (Snelling 1987:98). In other words, once the divide has been crossed there is no coming back.

The less rigorous response suggests that it is not personality which withers away, but the craving for the vain attachments of this life (the five 'Hindrances' and the ten 'Fetters'). What is overcome is not individuality as such, but self-inflicted suffering. Hence, it makes sense to commit oneself to the rigorous discipline which is necessary on the noble eightfold path. There has ultimately to be an 'I', which, however much detached from fleeting pleasures, false securities and imagined realities, can speak meaningfully about another world, a further shore, the end of a journey.

One would imagine that if Buddhists were absolutely consistent they would have to deal with the question of pluralism by denying its existence. The very notion of many beliefs, often conflicting with one another, is part of the unreality of the world which brings suffering. However, the path to enlightenment is difficult to tread, not least because, in the nature of the case, it contradicts daily living. Everyday life, tragically, is often about strife. Although Buddhism ought itself to turn away from such delusions of existence and concentrate on the means of eliminating the necessity for them – the sensuous and senseless craving for material objects which brings the conflict – in fact it cannot avoid being caught in the midst of the present struggle for a more just and human existence within the present cycle of existence. Thus Buddhists are engaged in seeking peace and reconciliation between warring communities in Sri Lanka. They are deeply and openly concerned about oppressive political regimes in Burma and Vietnam, and about foreign occupation in Tibet. In a word, whatever the teaching appears to say to the contrary, there is a deep and substantial ethical concern within Buddhist tradition.

The first of the ten 'Perfections' is generosity (*dana*). This can be said to be at the heart of Buddhist morality. It is both the means and the evidence of the reversal of egocentric accumulation. Conflict, whether between persons, families, communities or nations, almost always arises from the fear of loss. But for a person on the way of the Buddha deprivation is a positive gain, for it is the stripping away of illusory desire. To struggle, if necessary by force, to gain what one does not have is to lose what one needs most – detachment. Hence, generosity (as in Jesus' saying about the two coats – Mt. 5:40) is the antidote to enmity caused by a sense of affronted rights.

The last of the ten 'Perfections' is equanimity (*uppekha*). One cannot help wondering if this is not truer to the heart of the Buddhist world-view and, in point of fact, the end of morality:

> Equanimity is that ability to accept the vicissitudes of life calmly and dispassionately . . . This is not a numbed indifference or, still less, a neurotic dissociation from life. Rather it arises from seeing that *intrinsically all events are neutral* and that it is desire that picks and chooses, grades this as good and that as bad. *The bodhisatta sits comfortably in any set of conditions*; he is *immovably* at home

in the world, whatever befalls. (Snelling 1987:85, italics mine)

Here, perhaps, authentic Buddhism is speaking its true word of passivity and abstention.

UNITY, STRUGGLE AND LAW – ISLAM

With Islam we are transported into a different world. At the risk of dangerous over-simplification, the religion of Muslims appears to be guided by three fundamental principles: *tawhid* (unity), *jihad* (struggle) and *shariah* (law).

Tawhid represents a particular view of the world which demonstrates the unity of the whole of existence. This is not the kind of meta-historical unity represented by the flowing together of Brahman and Atman, nor the unity of pure-consciousness discovered in overcoming the appearance of unrelated diversity in the world of unreality. It is, historically speaking, first and foremost the unity of God which sets aside the polytheism of traditional religion in which each human group possesses its own god for its own benefit.

Islamic unity contradicts the antagonism caused within the human community, along racial, national, social, legal and genetic lines by the ignorance and perversity of human beings who do not recognise the revealed will of Allah as given through Muhammad, the last and seal of the prophets. Islamic unity also contradicts any attempt to separate the spiritual from the temporal, the religious from the secular, divine law from its embodiment in the laws of the nations.

The religious and political community are one and the same. The right path embraces the whole of life. The objective of Islam is the purification of the soul and the reconstruction of society by means of the code (*shariah*) revealed by God to Muhammad (Ahmad 1976:37). Islam accounts for itself as a 'guided tour' through life in which human beings can perfectly fulfil their destiny by listening to God's word (the Qur'an).

The Qur'an contains all necessary regulations for conduct. By the beginning of the third century after the *hijra* to Medina (c.900), a refining process of codification, following the initial work by Muhammad, resulted in an impressive system of jurisprudence. This work of codification is final. Henceforth Islamic law (or *shariah*) is a matter of interpreting and applying the original system. It is the state's responsibility, guided by the accredited religious authorities, to establish, maintain and develop virtue and eradicate those evils in the human community which God finds abhorrent.

Islam was born in struggle (*jihad*): firstly, the struggle for recognition and reform; secondly, the struggle for survival. One might interpret the history of Islam as the ascendency of the latter struggle (the lesser *jihad*) over the former (the greater *jihad*). Behind the struggle for survival was the intense consciousness that the new faith should not be allowed to fail. Hence, historically, Islam has often taken a militant attitude towards competitors (often Christianity).

Islam today would seem to be entering a fresh crisis of confidence and identity. It is engaged in what Akbar Ahmed (1988) calls its 'third encounter' with the West (the other two being with medieval and colonial Europe). It is an encounter in which freedom of belief, tolerance, democracy and an open society (in a word, plurality) have become not only aspirations of peoples all over the globe (Chile, Nicaragua, Sudan, South Africa, Nepal, Burma, Malaysia, Romania, Mongolia and many others), but the very conditions for survival.

Islam's difficulty is that its ideal, an Islamic state implementing *shariah* law, is a contradiction of the secular ideal of the complete separation of religion and political, legal and economic life. Can Muslims possibly give up their conviction of the indissoluble unity of religion and political power? Not as a temporary necessity for those living among the unbelievers, but as a matter of principled choice? Or are they to be among the last, along with some extreme

Hindu groups (unfortunately on the increase) in India and some Christian groups in the Lebanon and Northern Ireland, to maintain the enforced subordination of human life in society to absolute religious beliefs which many outside observers believe are being used as the means to avoid the dissolution of long-enjoyed political and civic privileges?

One interpretation of Islam's modern predicament is that throughout its history it has been more a civilisation and an empire than a religion. But now that the empire has long since gone and the civilisation is in a state of turmoil, only the religious part is left. However, for Islam religion without a republic is like a body without clothes; it is exposed and vulnerable.

What is at stake for Muslims living in the modern world is the very notion of an Islamic state. But no kind of theocracy in the history of the world, whatever the ideal may be, has ever been able to tolerate strong dissent and opposition. This has been true of the Roman Empire, its successor the Byzantine Empire, the early nation states of Europe, the changing empires of China and Japan and the communist and fascist states of the twentieth century. Only by loosening the theocratic ties between state and religion have people been free to express their real preferences and, whatever the ultimate reality of economic power, to have a sense of genuine political, social and individual choice.

A theocracy is almost bound in practice to silence its prophets. For Islam this would indeed be a paradox. The problem is that the ideal relationship, in which political life is subordinated to a set of high ethical values enshrined in religious belief (Muslims would say in the very utterances of God), usually becomes inverted in reality. Religion then becomes a tool whereby political power is seized and maintained. It is interpreted to fit the needs of those who happen to be in the political ascendency at any particular moment. Christendom is littered with painful examples of this process. Islam, too, has succumbed many times to the same process, as for example in the transition from the so-called 'ideal caliphs' to the Umayyad and Abbasid dynasties.

It has taken the Christian Church hundreds of years to learn that the experiment with theocracy is a vale of tears and a bed of suffering. It has caused immense misery and resentment, and is mainly to blame for the deep suspicion and caution that both Jews and Muslims in particular feel towards all Christian claims. Does Islam, then, have the resources within its own tradition to come to terms with a world whose peoples everywhere are embarked on their own *jihad* against all pretence to a monopoly of power? Inexorable social pressures in the modern world will surely squeeze out what for some may still remain the Islamic ideal.

Writing some time ago, Stephen Neill expressed his belief that 'the central question [for Islam] is whether it will remain a comprehensive culture based on a religion, or become a "church", a religious institution within a secular civilisation' (Neill 1961:56). This is no longer a question for Muslims living in the West, except in the unimaginable circumstances of there being a massive conversion to Islam, because Western societies are irretrievably pluralist both in fact and conviction, and could not therefore conceive of any religion ever again becoming the sole formative influence on their moral values, lifestyles, customs or goals. Increasingly, theocracy is not much of an option even in nations where the majority are Muslims. Whatever religious leaders may desire to be the case, commitment to plurality and pragmatism (even by an as-yet 'silent majority') is a very powerful urge in our contemporary world. We will be exploring both the positive and negative aspects of plurality and pluralism later on. Prior to that we will examine the thesis that the Christian religion is a subtle, and not always easily recognisable, perversion of the original message of Jesus and his apostles.

The purpose of this chapter has been to look briefly at some of the main characteristics of the four most significant world religions in relation to the immense pressure of modern Westernised culture to confine their place of operation to the private spheres of life. We have noticed too that this challenge cannot be avoided, painful as it may be for religions as ancient as the ones touched upon.

Leaders of these faiths will have to learn to cope with the tension between maintaining a largely unbroken identity inherited from centuries of commonly accepted beliefs and practices and the need to adapt to a fast-changing, competitive world in which the younger members of their communities are constantly being subjected to the possibility of choosing alternative beliefs and lifestyles to those their parents hold to. In the future the worth and durability of a particular set of beliefs may well be proven largely by its ability to deal with both the substance of the irreligious critique of faith, which has come from the thinking of Marx, Nietzsche and Freud, and what today we call the reality of modernity – the assumptions, translated into action, of a culture indifferent to religion, hostile to any claims to final truth, self-confident in the power of technology to solve social and environmental problems, opposed to authoritarian constraints on freedom and orientated to the pursuit of happiness through individual self-fulfilment and self-gratification.

For all these world religions, though in different measures, this struggle is still largely for the future. In this they differ from the Christian faith, which has had to struggle long and hard, already for two hundred years or more, to avoid being buried by an avalanche of 'anti-faith' which in some senses it was itself instrumental in setting off.

5

Christianity Among the Religions

'In inter-religious discussion real decisions are made at the beginning of the argument, not at the end.'

—**Lesslie Newbigin**

'The Hindu is not an object for conversion. He or she is a fellow-pilgrim with whom we share the decisive impact Christ has had on our lives.'

—**Wesley Ariarajah**

'I am sending you to them to open their eyes and turn them from darkness to light, and from the power of Satan to God.'

—**Jesus to Paul on the Damascus Road**

Coexistence, dialogue or mission?

Christians who regularly meet people of different religions and are involved in discussions with them often remind the Church that it has to come to terms with the multi-cultural nature of all modern societies. It can no longer live as if the Christian faith was superior to all the others which jostle beside it for recognition and respect.

The great missionary conference held in Edinburgh in 1910, to which the overwhelming number of delegates were

Western Christians, has been described as a watershed, the end of an illusion that all the nations of the world would, through the preaching of the gospel, bow the knee to Jesus Christ. Four years later the outbreak of the so-called 'Great War', which showed cynical disregard for human life, the incompetence of European leaders, the hunger for power and the final vindictive humiliation of the German people, shattered beyond all recovery the arrogant assumptions of Western superiority, grounded in the Christian faith.

There are many other reasons why the peoples of the West need to learn humility and open themselves to learning from other peoples and their cultures: the Jewish Holocaust, the absence (until recently) of religious and political freedom in the nations of Eastern Europe, the willingness, if necessary, to start a nuclear war. But an even truer indication of the corruption of the vaunted European civilisation is the conquest and subjugation of the colonies, first by military power, now by economic means.

IN ALL THINGS, PLURALISM

However vital these realities are in considering the relation between different beliefs across the world, they are not the main reason why some are strongly cautioning the Christian Church against trying to persuade those outside to come in. The more fundamental reason is the full acceptance of the assumptions of a relativistic view of life, as we outlined it in chapter 3. Familiar slogans would be: 'To every culture its own religion'; 'To every belief its own portion of the truth'; 'Where there appears to be disagreement, exercise tolerance and patience until we can bring them together in a higher synthesis.'

Theological pluralism is being persuasively advocated by a number of influential figures. Among those, we could mention Wilfred Cantwell Smith, Stanley Samartha, Paul Knitter, Wesley Ariarajah, John Hick, Kim Yong-Bock, Alan Race, Raymond Panikkar. Although there are different ways of stating the case, the central thesis of the 'pluralists' is that God is equally at work in all religious traditions, bringing people to ultimate salvation. This being so, evangelistic activity on the part of Christians, outside the nominal of their own faith, is a tacit denial of what God is about. God has disclosed himself, admittedly in different ways, to all peoples. The various religions are the result of people's apprehension of his footsteps among them.

Because the arguments are being widely canvassed, are having a considerable impact on some sections of the Church, and appear to run counter to mainstream Christian opinion down the ages, we will try to look very carefully at the assumptions on which they are based. Obviously, the place from which a person starts a journey will largely determine the route taken. The chosen destination will also limit the choice of roads. Once on the journey, where we think we are will dictate how we proceed on our way. Whence? Where? Whither? These are three ways in which we might tackle these assumptions.

The starting-place

Arising from observation of what has been happening, I detect two overriding convictions that have set the pluralists out on their journey of exploration. They argue that as we look around us we notice firstly that, contrary to what former generations of Christians expected to happen, people of other faiths have not abandoned their beliefs and customs and turned to Christ and the Church in large numbers. The vast majority of people living on this planet today will be born, live and die in exactly the same set of beliefs. It is therefore mischievous to imagine that their hope of final bliss depends on the ability of Christian missionaries to persuade them to change their fundamental convictions for others which seem distant and alien.

Secondly, the pluralists say that we may also notice how the description which other people give of their experience of a transcendent, divine being is remarkably similar to that experienced by Christians. Their view is that, apparently without knowledge of the gospel, these people have come to know God truly. Many seem to experience his grace and forgiveness and demonstrate a life in accordance with his holy and loving purposes.

Our present address

What are the main assumptions today's pluralists make?

In the area of language, which we have already discussed, four principles seem to be operating. Firstly, all statements about God are assumed to be limited, if not defective and misleading. Secondly, our view of God can no longer be Christocentric: Jesus Christ cannot be regarded as the one true and definitive measure of what God is like. Thirdly, there must always be a 'fuller vision and richer understanding of God' (King 1986:14). Finally, what we do not know now about God we will discover in the diverse traditions of other faiths, or in a common search for the ultimate reality beyond all our partial glimpses of it.

The actual result of these assumptions is that conversation about God is inevitably marked by vagueness, moving in the direction of an impersonal, rather than personal, view of the transcendent. In so far as the latter is deprecated as requiring too definite a perspective on God, the result is far from pluralist. It amounts to a commitment to an impersonal view of final reality.

Another aspect of the language question is the assumption that God's self-disclosure through his word should not be over-emphasised. In her comments on the Hindu concept of *darshan* ('seeing'), Ursula King believes that too much emphasis on our senses (particularly hearing) may well be more of a hindrance than a help in moving towards the divine. There are other variants of the same assumption. Thus, Demetrios Constantelos (1981) believes that what is claimed to be God's word is more likely to be the community reflecting on its own history in its own interest. It is only hearing an echo of its own voice projected on to the heavens. Wilfred Cantwell Smith, in a very well-rehearsed and oft-repeated argument (Hick and Hebblethwaite 1980:87–107), maintains that revelation is not fundamentally propositional (i.e., it does not come through verbal statements), but personal (i.e., it comes through people and their actions). Behind these negative judgements on the ability of words to convey knowledge of God and his ways is one of the main assumptions of the old liberal Protestant subjectivism: language about God reflects human beings' faltering attempts to capture in verbal images their immediate experience of God.

A further assumption about God in the context of other faiths is the need to move away from a theology of salvation to one of creation (see e.g., Roy Pape in Cracknell and Lamb 1986). Prior to advancing and defending theories about how God saves in this life (or in the life to come), we should understand how other religions fit into God's purposes. This necessity springs from the assumption that, contrary to the Christian Church's two-millennial obsession with the problem of evil, the real question to be faced has to do with goodness. Where do saintly lives come from? The obvious answer is that they flow from the well-spring of God's grace, beyond a conscious recognition of Christ as the only saviour of the world.

It is axiomatic for the pluralist that specific historical happenings cannot be the vehicle for an exclusive manifestation of God. Visser 't Hooft (1963:90) quotes Aldous Huxley's pungent criticism of Christianity for its 'idolatrous preoccupation with events and things in time – events and things regarded not merely as useful means, but as ends, intrinsically sacred and indeed divine'. The assumption behind this judgement goes all the way back to the metaphysical dualism which probably originated in Mesopotamia and spread west to Greece and east to India. Matter, being evil, cannot be the pure vehicle through which the divine is able to come to us and we are able to ascend to the divine. In the West this common viewpoint finds its most powerful presenter in Immanuel Kant (1724–1804), who stressed that the really real is found in the realm of ideas.

In the German tradition of existentialist theology a radical distinction is drawn between historical fact, which may be uncovered by historical investigation, and historical meaning. This distinction has been developed in two ways. Firstly, there is no necessary connection between the historical event (thought of as bare fact) and the meaning which is ascribed to it in the tradition. Thus the confession that Jesus is alive is in no way dependent on the fact that the tomb was empty on the first Easter morning. Secondly, there is no necessary connection between the original meaning given to the story and the meaning it has for me today. If I happen to be an inheritor of the Christian tradition, the Jesus story may illuminate how I understand and react to the world today, but to someone standing within another history it might have little or nothing to say.

The desired destination

The final set of assumptions has to do with the way the pluralist would like to see the discussion going. Foremost among them is the desire that Christians will substantially alter their understanding of Jesus. Clearly the historical, orthodox view of Christ is the major roadblock in the way of a pluralist vision of other religions. If the Christian's interpretation of the Christ-event remains basically the same as it has always been, there can be little hope of *rapprochement* with people of other faiths. Muslims, for example, do not believe that God could have allowed so special a prophet to have died. Jews cannot accept that God's kingdom is present with Jesus. Hindus refuse to acknowledge only one, normative appearance of God. For Buddhists the cause of suffering is not real and personal evil in the universe, therefore its overcoming cannot be through the voluntary suffering of an innocent man.

There have been many and varied attempts to 'reinterpret' Jesus Christ in a way which would remove the scandal of his particularity, or, even more subtly, to reinterpret that particularity in a way which other faiths would find acceptable. Behind all the discussions about what Jesus Christ could become for people of other faiths lies the most basic assumption of all: it is imperative for us to find ways of describing or commending him other than in the rigid categories of New Testament Christology. Paul Knitter (1985:chs 9–10) is the one most explicit in his demand for the right and freedom to interpret Christ in non-exclusive terms. We are given, he believes, the responsibility of evolving Christologies in ways which do justice to the plurality of views about Christ, so that he may become a means of unity among people, not a continuing cause of division.

This being the undeniable motivating force behind the pluralist urge to reinterpret, all the attempts made and the arguments adduced are inevitably contrived and artificial. They lack any real historical credibility (as we will later go on to show). Of course, an authentic pluralist would not be particularly disturbed by this since, ultimately, the important question is not: Who was (and therefore is) this Jesus 'who was put to death by . . . the cross' and 'raised . . . from the dead' (Acts 2:23–4)? but: Who can this Jesus become for us with our new historical consciousness of the relativity of all cultures and historical achievements? (Knitter 1985:173).

Bearing in mind, then, that there is a dogmatic need, every bit as unyielding as any refusal to compromise the orthodox doctrine of Christ, to change our traditional image of Christ, we will survey some of the strategies which are adopted.

Firstly, there is recourse to the so-called historical-critical method of approach to the Gospels. This may proceed in a number of different directions. It is claimed, for example, that Jesus never thought of himself as God in human flesh. He was conscious of being a special agent for the inauguration of God's kingdom, but not of being divine in an ontological sense. The language of divinity was added by the early Church to the primitive tradition as the only way the disciples could describe the impact which Jesus had had on their lives. Today we, who know how this type of mythological language works, should understand the titles given to Jesus as symbols of his quality of life, or his unsurpassed grasp of God's will, or his authority in reinterpreting the Jewish faith, or his willingness to suffer the ultimate consequence of his option for the oppressed poor. This means that he has no absoluteness in himself as a person, but only in what he represents.

Another line of argument is to suggest that Jesus' own theocentric view of the world was converted by the early Church to a Christocentric view. Extravagant claims for Jesus were forced upon the Church by the need to survive in a hostile world. As a young, inexperienced and unprotected community it needed to defend itself against the many lords and many gods of the ancient Mediterranean world. Today the Church does not need to be defensive in relation to other religions. It should, then, adopt more inclusive Christologies.

Pluralists, like all who want to take other religions seriously, have to try to give an account of the biblical passages which appear to interpret Christ's person and work as utterly unique and unrepeatable. As their *a priori* presuppositions will not allow them to take the passages at face value, 'unique' too is given some subtle twists. For example, Jesus is unique in the sense that all great teachers and prophets are. There is simply nobody like him in any other tradition. But, then, there is nobody like the others either. In this sense we may affirm that Jesus is Lord, but so also are Krishna, the Buddha, and so on. Or, Jesus is unique because, in a way in which (naturally) no one else could be, he 'remains the source of knowledge and truth about God for Christians' (King 1986:14). Or, he is unique in giving us a singular insight into God as Father, one central but not exclusive view of God. Or, finally, he is unique in his apprehension of the future transformation of the world. Like no other, he was able to anticipate in his public ministry the coming liberation of creation in which all things would become new.

We can mention one other line of Christological enquiry which is popular among pluralists and, to be fair, among others who do not share their excessively relativising enthusiasms. We refer to the ancient and noble tradition which sees Christ as the Logos (or God's Word) who is not limited either to the New Testament or to the Christian community. The same Word which became manifest openly and publicly in Jesus Christ has spoken in and through other holy people, perhaps in a more hidden, less tangible way. Nevertheless, it is because the seed of the Word has been scattered abroad across the face of the earth that people can and do come to know and reverence God, lead lives of purity and honesty, and work for the welfare of others.

PLURALISM DOES NOT WORK

As Knitter (1985) so openly confesses, theological pluralism beautifully fits the mood of our times. Because it is ultimately pragmatic in tone and in intention, not wanting to pose such embarrassing questions as those about truth, it is also highly seductive. Like relativism, I believe, it is not so much misguided as impossible. I will now try to show why this is inevitably the case.

The wrong end of the stick

To begin with, it would be good to clear away some possible misunderstandings. I would like to state clearly what is not at stake in my criticism of the position I have been describing. This is particularly important because, when discussing pluralism, people can easily pass one another like ships in the night, misinterpreting where the argument is leading.

Firstly, I would not dare to speculate about any person's ultimate relationship to the living God. Trying to play at God is idolatry. All I can say is that if God is like Jesus Christ, a person's salvation will not depend on the intensity of their search, righteous life, strength of faith, achievements in prayer or dedication to serving the needy – in a word, on religion. Though all these aspects of a person's spiritual life are important, they are not a path *to* God, but a path *out from* him. The one and only possible way of encountering God is through his own initiative, in which in his grace he lovingly calls us to abandon our own strivings after truth, reality and purity, in order to be able to accept his free gift of salvation.

Then, secondly, God's activity among all human beings is not at stake either. Again, to seek to confine God's work of grace would be presumptuous idolatry. Though not yet children of God's kingdom, for they have not come to recognise God as their Abba, Father, many people are actively engaged, whether they are conscious of it or not, as agents of the kingdom. Their work of caring, nurturing, healing, reconciling, opposing violence and injustice is a sign of the reversal of evil in this world order. Whether or not they subscribe to any particular religious or ideological belief, they are manifesting in their lives a recognition that, in God's world, it is more blessed to give than to receive. They are prompted to this work of mercy and justice by God's Spirit. One should rejoice and praise God for every manifestation of goodness.

Thirdly, the imperative for dialogue with people of other faiths is not at stake either. In Christian circles dialogue has become an emotive word, a slogan and a means of accusing those who hold to a different view of other religions than one's own. For me, basically, dialogue is the meeting of people who are willing to share themselves and their convictions and to receive from the other whatever he or she wants to bring. There are no preconditions, apart from the commitment to honesty and total respect for the other person's humanity. Nor are any particular results ruled out in advance. Thus, for example, dialogue which cannot issue in deep changes of belief and lifestyle is no more than an unreal ritual. In this sense it is neither an alternative to, nor necessarily a preplanned means for, evangelism.

The right end of the stick

On the other hand, there are two further vitally important pluralist assumptions which cannot escape criticism.

The first is that religions as such are manifestations of

God at work. This is a curious idea, for if all religions somehow reflect the reality of the divine being, it would be a strange God indeed who existed. Would he be a God whose unity was postulated in a precise mathematical way, or whose unity could be expressed in diversity of being? Would he be a God whose power is manifested by suffering himself the opposition of the world, or by stamping it out by destroying his enemies, or by teaching that it is only an appearance of an unreal existence? The notion that 'no religion is absolute, only God is absolute' is banal. How can we talk at all about this absolute God except by discussing the incredibly varied descriptions we have of him in the different faiths?

The second assumption at stake is that every religion is a path to God. However, unless there is a common mind about the nature of the goal, we can know neither the destination nor whether we are on the right path. That is axiomatic for any kind of pilgrimage. If a Muslim and a Christian meet at London Airport, one on a Hajj to Mecca and the other going to Jerusalem to celebrate Easter there, the pilots of the respective planes would think them charmingly ignorant if they thought they would end up in the same place.

1. This brings us to one of our main objections to the pluralist thesis. It has to do with the age-old problem of knowing. Whatever pluralists may say about other people's claims to know, or be known by, the truth, their own has to be unquestioned, otherwise their whole case collapses. What they claim to know is that it would be unfair (and inefficient) for God to confide his truth to only one people and to manifest himself in only one history.

How do they know this? Well, several answers could be given. The empirical evidence would point overwhelmingly to a number of simultaneous revelations in different parts of the world. Yet, this argument is a non-starter unless one has already accepted one manifestation as a norm by which to discern all the others.

Another possibility would be an overwhelming religious

consensus about the answers to the great enigmas of life. But religions do not have the same answers; they do not even have the same questions!

A third way might be through intuition, or through a sublime mystical experience, whereby we 'perceive' inwardly that all things are one. Such experiences are fine, but they set apart the person concerned from the rest of humanity as infallible. This is not the normal way that we know anything or any person. On what grounds, then, is religious truth made into a complete exception?

The final possibility would be through one of the religions concerned; that is, that there has been a definitive and authoritative disclosure that all beliefs are part of a truth far more immense than any one of them. Here we come to the nub of the question, because this is precisely what some religions do claim. But others, most notably Christianity, clearly do not – unless, of course, they are reinterpreted out of all recognition. In other words, whether consciously or not, the pluralist has already accepted the presuppositions of one way of looking at reality. So, for example, as Roger Hooker (1989:365) says, 'Cantwell Smith's view of cultural relativism is very close to what some contemporary Hindus themselves urge upon us.'

2. Our second main objection to pluralism is that it excludes Christianity, and therefore cannot be truly pluralist. Put another way, Christianity can only be included in the dream of a common religious path by disowning its own self-confessed identity. Though apparently unrelenting in its claim to final revelation, even Islam, in its doctrine of the former prophets sent to all nations and in its affirmation of 'natural religion', allows a certain pluralism. Not so the faith of Jesus Christ. Christian exclusivism at the point of religion (I reiterate, not at the point of God's work among people) is not based, as some want to imagine, on selected verses and passages from the Old and New Testaments. Though the natural sense of such verses as John 14:6 and Acts 4:12 is powerful in its advocacy of 'only one way', the biblical view of religion does not hinge on isolated texts.

In general terms, the biblical writers point to the way in which sin has corrupted every human enterprise. They are particularly critical of the way in which perfectly legitimate pursuits have been manipulated for selfish interests. Even God-given structures like the law, or provisions like the land, have been turned into weapons of deceit, exploitation and self-righteousness. According to the biblical world-view, at the root of the human predicament is the drive to become independent of whatever we consider limits our freedom, namely the constraints of the world as God has made it. As a result we have, in innumerable ways, exchanged the real world for one of our own creating. This is the real meaning of idolatry, far more subtle and sinister than any external manifestation in terms of religious rites and customs. Religion, as such, is but one (though admittedly the most significant) of the many structures which humans have created in order to make sense of a world they have exchanged for the real one.

Religion, to use the Marxist terminology, is part of the superstructure which reflects an alienated existence. For the Bible, that alienation is not only from our own humanity and from our fellow humans, but much more fundamentally from God. Now this does not mean, any more than it does in the case of other structures (like economics, politics, the arts, family life), that the whole of religious life is utterly depraved. That is not the question: undoubtedly there is much in some people's religious life which is wholesome and right. The point is that religion as a whole, as a way of interpreting life, misconceives the real world. It is based on an illusion about final reality.

The gospel of Jesus Christ is based on the assumption that there is a world which is passing away and a new one which is coming into existence. Religion as such belongs to the old world. It is part of what crucified the Lord of glory (1 Cor. 2:8). Nevertheless, from within it, here and there, appear the fresh green shoots of the new which manifest the witness of himself which God has left with all people (Acts 14:17; 17:27–8). This is the reason why the gospel of

Christ (over against the Christian religion) can never be co-opted for the pluralist view. Without it, however, pluralism has rather lost its clothes.

There are further reasons why pluralism is bound to exclude Christian faith. We can spell them out briefly, though there is not the space to elaborate them in any detail.

Firstly, the Christian view of God entails the Christian understanding of incarnation. Because the whole earth which God has made is good and beautiful, there is nothing incongruous in God himself enjoying it, not from afar off, but in its midst. All the language of God coming down, of walking in the garden, of appearing to Abraham, Joshua and others is not mere naive anthropomorphism. It is a perfectly natural deduction from who God is. Moreover, human beings are like God, they are created in his image; what could be more reasonable, then, that God should become as one of them? This fact is forcefully expressed in Colossians 1:15: 'He [Jesus Christ, as man] is the [visible] image of the invisible God.' It would indeed be strange if the God whose picture we have in the story of Israel did not come among us in the one way which really makes sense: like each one of us, a unique and particular person. In the same way, continuing the same line of thought, it is not surprising that the ultimate reality of Hindu faith should be manifested in many 'incarnations'. They are not equivalent happenings, for the view of the ultimate represented by them is not equivalent to the biblical view of God's relationship to creation.

The second reason for the exclusion of Christian faith concerns the New Testament's portrayal of Jesus Christ. The only way of making Jesus Christ inclusive for the religions of the world is by trying to fit him into an alien framework. However ingenious their interpretation, and however implicitly honourable may be their intention, the attempts of people like Ariarajah, Cracknell and Knitter to forge a non-traditional Christology out of the New Testament must be suspect. The fact that, to support their case for a less assertive doctrine of Christ, they need to discover certain elements in the text and eliminate others means that the conclusions are already contained in the premises. Hence, dealing straightforwardly with certain texts without resorting to special pleading proves exceedingly problematical.

Cracknell's handling of Acts 4:12 (1986:108) is a good case in point. Firstly, he suggests that the word for salvation could be translated 'healing', though he does admit that the usual translation is the most likely. Secondly, he asserts that 'St. Peter is not making a general statement of universal validity but is appealing to the Jewish leaders that such a healing is reason for them to accept their Messiah.' Both these points are taken as reasons for throwing doubt on the view that this verse gives enough grounds for 'an exclusive view about who is ultimately acceptable to God'.

Naturally, evidence that the first Christians believed that Jesus Christ alone was God's appointed means of salvation does not depend on stringing together isolated texts here and there. That would be a very unsophisticated way of handling the New Testament! The evidence is in the consistent way in which the New Testament writers bring together the nature and action of God, the meaning of Christ's death and resurrection, and human needs. It would have been inconceivable to them that God would send his only Son as a perfect sacrifice for the sin of the whole world, and then accept other ways of salvation which had no reference to this finished work.

The point at issue for Cracknell seems to be that, *a priori*, exclusive claims for Christ vitiate a genuine dialogue with people of other faiths. Therefore, the text *has to be* reinterpreted so that the 'name of Jesus' becomes 'the grace and love which Jesus represents', which then 'might be found under the names of the other religious traditions' (Cracknell 1986:109). The basis of the dialogue, then, is not the most natural meaning of the text, but its subtle reinterpretation.

Christian faith and truth

The arguments against pluralism bring us to one final point: how should we evaluate the very fundamental question of truth, and in particular the claims made by the biblical writers to know the truth? The subject is vast, controversial and complex. I have already surveyed some aspects of the debate. Here I would like to make three points briefly by way of continuing the debate and setting the scene for the chapters which follow.

THE UNPOPULARITY OF TRUTH

There are two serious general misunderstandings about truth. One is that, because as finite and flawed human beings we cannot grasp truth finally or perfectly, our understanding must always be tentative, uncertain and ambivalent. Like the canny fish that always eludes our rod and line, truth is forever beyond our reach. The more we think we have it the more it swims away. The other is that claims to know the truth are the height of arrogance and presume a judgemental attitude on all who disagree.

Of course, it is true that we are finite beings and therefore we could not possibly have anything more than a limited grasp of truth. It is equally true that we are flawed by self-deception and confusion, and therefore we may easily get a distorted view of many things. Neither of these facts, however, hinder us completely from the possibility of knowing a part of what is absolutely true, and knowing it without misrepresentation.

The Christian claim is that truth comes by means of God communicating something to us (cf. Jn. 1:17; 14:6; 16:13; 17:17; 18:37; 2 Cor. 4:2; Eph. 1:13; 2 Tim. 2:15). There is nothing absurd about that. He could hardly be God, and we certainly could not be creatures in his image, if he could not enable us to receive reliably what he wanted to give us. The analogy between two human beings is almost exact: we believe that we can gain an accurate, though obviously not complete, picture of another person by what they tell us of themselves. There is, however, one major difference in the analogy: by nature, God cannot deceive us. Unlike us, he does not try to project an image, only his true self.

If truth comes ultimately from God, it is not arrogant to believe it, rather it is arrogant not to believe it. The claim that all perception of truth is relative is a claim about truth – and is based on a personal presumption, whose source is one's own authority, that this must be the case. What could be more arrogant than that?

KNOWING THE TRUTH

Biblically, knowing the truth has three dimensions. There is no necessary chronological order, for they are inextricably bound up together. According to the circumstances, one or another will start the procedure.

Hearing

We are able to apprehend the truth because God has spoken. Given the fact that we live for a short time and are severely limited in our capacity to learn from the accumulated wisdom of the ages, it is clear that the truth about the ultimate things of life – the beginning and end of all things, who we are and for what purpose we exist at all – must come to us from outside our own experience, and in an accessible form. If the universe was silent (as modern artists and philosophers have often affirmed), we could know little or nothing about that truth which really matters.

It has become almost a truism in much modern theology that God does not reveal himself in propositional form, but in personal terms. This kind of dichotomy reveals a very basic confusion, which if applied to ordinary daily life would make a nonsense of our experience. Of course, God's supreme and final revelation of truth is Jesus Christ, according to the saying 'grace and truth came through Jesus Christ'

(Jn. 1:17). The one who has seen Jesus Christ has seen the Father (Jn. 14:9). However, we would not know what the truth is about unless, along with the bare fact of Jesus' existence, statements were made which conveyed the meaning. Hence, the one who became flesh and dwelt among us was also the eternal Word. He was life, which the disciples saw with their own eyes and touched. But he was also the Word of life, whom they heard with their own ears (1 Jn. 1:1). If the truth does not come in propositions, it does not come at all. Without words we could make no sense of it. Jesus Christ is proclaimed, therefore, as the one who has told the truth which he has heard from God (Jn. 8:40). God's word is truth (Jn. 17:17).

Choosing

In spite of the importance of the word, it goes without saying that knowledge of the truth does not come through the theoretical grasp of abstract statements about ultimate reality. Truth is about life, and life is more than the intellect. Truth to be known has to be believed, and belief means the commitment of the whole of one's being to the message which is heard. Hence, the solemn call to choose between life and death (Deut. 30:19), or to choose between God and Baal (1 Kings 18:21), is inescapable. Not to choose is still a commitment; and it is one which may make it more difficult to distinguish between the truth and counterfeits.

Acting

Truth has to be heard, believed with one's whole being, and tested in practice. It is equally important for the biblical view that truth is something we do. It is an active engagement: if the message you are hearing is true, you must do something about it. Merely to hear and assent is not to know the truth. God's truth is life-transforming, and therefore it can only be known as it is practised. It is fully grasped 'along the way'.

The Christian view rejects false alternatives: truth is both personal and propositional; truth is both received in the mind and carried out in action by the will; truth both comes to us from an independent source outside and is made ours in our own experience.

THE NEW GNOSTICS

A final word of caution. Just as objective claims to know the truth are unpopular, so the internal path of subjective experience is extremely fashionable. Of course, they are the two sides of the same coin. If there is nothing to hear from elsewhere, there is no alternative but to listen to ourselves. This is said to come through a process of reflection which may take many different forms, principally those of body control (through physical techniques like yoga and breathing exercises) and of meditation. Behind the process lies the assumption that there is a layer of false consciousness that has to be broken through, in order to be able to reach a new level of consciousness, which is the real self. Release from the appearances of reality comes through knowledge, awareness and enlightenment. The problem of truth is resolved by overcoming the ignorance within.

Although this view of truth is increasingly popular among a population that is almost wholly alienated from even the echo of Christian faith, it does not resolve the fundamental problem of reality. Is there any way of being certain that techniques of meditation do not lead us from one degree of unreality to another? How could we distinguish between the real me and a fantasy world? Only, presumably, by trusting the judgement of a spiritual guide. But is he or she any wiser? They may make large claims, and yet they could simply be further along the road to total illusion. The frightening reality is that we could never know.

6

Jesus Christ Outside Religion

'Intellectually, religious emotions are not creative, but conservative. They attach themselves readily to the current view of the world and consecrate it.'

—**John Dewey**

'We have been dosing our people with religion when what they need is not that but the living God.'

—**Frederick D. Maurice**

'What matters in the Church is not religion but the form of Christ.'

—**Dietrich Bonhoeffer**

'It was Jesus' view that repentance was hardest for the pious man, because he was separated from God not by crude sins, but by his piety. Nothing separates a man from God so radically as self-assured piety.'

—**Joachim Jeremias**

Christianity in the world today

There is no reason on earth why any religion should expect to occupy a privileged place in the modern world and be shielded from a questing and critical investigation. In one sense – which later will be substantially qualified – Christianity is a religion like any other. At least that is how it has appeared concretely in history, with its institutions, rituals, traditions, professional leadership, conditions for membership, considerable influence on culture and society, and distinctive doctrines.

For better or worse, Christianity has been largely identified with the history of Europe, at least since the time of the Emperor Constantine. Even before that, the early 'Fathers' of the Church taught and wrote in and for an environment heavily influenced by the thinking of Greek philosophy. There can be no question that, whatever the theoretical response to the question, 'What has Athens to do with Jerusalem?', in practice it had much.

Conceivably the history of the Christian faith might have been written differently. Early Christian missionaries, including some of the apostles, travelled to Arabia, Persia, Armenia, Egypt, Ethiopia, India and China. There Christian communities were formed. Some withered and died, but others continued down the ages, though sadly cut off from the churches in Europe. With the coming of Islam in the early seventh century, and its swift military conquest of most of the territory from the North African Atlantic coast to the borders of India, the churches there suffered further isolation.

The development of Christianity into the modern world would surely have been very different if, instead of becoming the official religion of the conquering powers, it had remained, as in the first three centuries, a *religio non licita* (not a recognised religion). The story of the oriental churches, harassed for many centuries by the religion of another empire, is completely different. It needs to be better known, so that the witness of these churches may be allowed to counter-balance the predominant faith of Christendom.

History can be rewritten, but it cannot be remade. The Christian faith today, even in its phenomenal spread in the last two centuries to every corner of the globe, is still largely the product of its European past. Once perceptions become filed away over a long period of time in the collective memory of the community it is extremely hard to change them.

We can single out two mammoth effects of the European inheritance which continue to shape, and in the opinion of an increasing number of Christians to distort, the life and witness of the Christian Church worldwide. The first is its long association with political and economic power. The second is its strong inclination to accept a radical divorce between spiritual and material reality, between the sacred and the secular, between the world to come and the present one. In general terms the power complex comes from Europe's Roman past, while the dualism comes from the Greeks.

These two effects have radically altered the way Christianity has come to be rooted in human communities. They give some credence to the perhaps too simplistic notion that the conversion of Constantine signalled the conversion of the Church to paganism. At least, it is relatively easy to trace a marked change in self-identity between the Church as the object of oppressive power and as a sharer in that power. The change has led to a long and unresolved debate within the Christian community about the exercise of power. Whatever had happened historically, the Church would still have needed to come to terms with the implications of power in witnessing to the gospel. However, the historical reality has moulded, and continues to mould, the response in subtle ways that do not seem to lessen with the passing of the generations.

The history of the European Church can be written in terms of the way in which throne and altar become enmeshed and groups of Christians reacted against this entanglement. It would, then, be easy to concentrate on the manner in which the Church accumulated for itself huge wealth or used the instruments of the state to persecute those who would not conform to its teaching and discipline. The Inquisition of the sixteenth century, the subjugation of the indigenous peoples of Central and South America in the same period, and the religious wars of the seventeenth century are telling reminders of what can happen when religious fanaticism and corrupt power are united. The Church also refused to let go its power in its disastrous and unnecessary clash with the new discoveries of the natural sciences from the sixteenth century onwards.

In the territorial expansion of the European powers the Church was there to legitimate and bless the conquest of land, industries, markets and souls. It also found little difficulty in justifying the massive loss of life for the sake of king (or kaiser) and country. In much more recent years groups of Christians have tended to glorify socialist revolutions, applying to them theological language like resurrection to new life from the dead. Equally, other groups have trumpeted the praises of brutal military regimes that have come to 'rescue' the people from the red tide which nearly engulfed them.

Looking at church history in terms of the way power has been abused, one might be excused a touch of cynicism. I believe that would be absolutely justified. To try to excuse the appalling record of the Church would be literally to add insult to injury – insult to intelligence, injury to the millions who have suffered. However, this is by no means the whole story. It would be easy, and possibly also a symptom of one's desire to have power – this time over the Christian faith by being able to dismiss it – to highlight only the dark side of the Church's history. This would be to forget, firstly, the many examples of resistance to the predominant thirst for authority and conformity – the Franciscans, the Benedictines, the Waldenses, Wyclif and the Lollards, the Mennonites and the Moravians, even the Jesuits in some of their actions in South America to defend the indigenous peoples against the Spanish land-owning aristocracy. Secondly, it would be to forget that those who suffered the abuse of power were themselves confessing disciples of Christ. At least until the end of the Thirty Years War (1648), but in many cases into the nineteenth century, Christian minorities were persecuted and discriminated against. The Church of Jesus Christ, divided against itself, was also a martyr Church within its own home.

The Church of the West is still strong. Its numerical decline has not necessarily affected its ability to control considerable financial and human resources within Third World countries. At least to some extent, evangelistic and development activity in the poorer nations has conjured up some of the colonialist ghosts of the past. Nevertheless, the growth of Christianity among the poor of the world has begun to bring a new consciousness of the task of the Church in renouncing power and its dualistic view of salvation in favour of seeking first God's kingdom of righteousness and justice among the people (more of that later). The emerging Church of the poor is challenging the Church of the privileged to end its long, uncritical association with the principalities of this present age.

Christianity as a religion

The process of conformity to the dominant assumptions of European culture has made of Christian faith what originally it arose in opposition to: another religion. We will try to unearth some of the principal characteristics of this conversion.

I will take as my starting-point some of the affirmations made about religion in the first two chapters, in order to see in what ways Christianity has fallen prey to what all critics of religion would consider a general disease. For the sake of brevity and, I hope, clarity, they can be divided into three separate groupings: religion used as an instrument to bring benefits and blessings upon the individual or community; religion used as a means of justifying and strengthening ethnic aspirations and sentiments; religion used to sanctify a given order and to be a refuge against change and upheaval.

RELIGION, THE TALISMAN

In many ways Christianity has fallen prey to those who believe that in its rites and prayers lie hidden untapped sources of beneficial power. Where Christianity has in times past been coextensive with a given population it has been virtually the only contender as a way of protection against unknown forces and unexpected catastrophes. Many people's expectation that their vulnerable baby has an inalienable right to be 'christened' according to the rite of the established Church, in order to place it within the realm of the morally good and spiritually healthy, is a residual inheritance of the Christendom of the past. Today, of course, there are many alternative religious practices which may be judged to offer similar power and protection.

Religion is largely perceived as an offer of safety against misfortune, help in time of trouble and comfort when suffering from physical ailments, emotional pressures or psychological distress. It is marked by the relative absence of corresponding obligations, except in so far as they are deemed necessary to secure the benefits. This accounts for the general willingness of parents to attend church services and preparation classes before baptism, but widespread reluctance to become involved in the life of the Church once the rite has been performed.

We should not think, however, that the talisman view of religion is largely confined to the 'hatched', 'matched' and 'dispatched' brigade. It is very much more subtle than that. Even among the Church's most enthusiastic supporters, belief and worship can easily become a comforting escape from the harshness and perplexity of modern secular life and an evasion of personal responsibilities. Though sometimes in danger of implying that they have a monopoly on renewal, people in the charismatic stream of contemporary church life tend to fall into the trap of religiosity. Then, freedom in worship can be a compensation for a deep feeling of being determined in the rest of life by circumstances outside one's control. Reliance on the immediate inner voice of God telling us what to do next with our lives may be a substitute for the hard rational and prayerful weighing up of alternatives and the willingness to wait for certainty, or even to live with uncertainty.

There are other ways in which the Christian religion can be subtly used as an unjustifiable compensation for not facing the truth about ourselves and the world that surrounds us. For example, our patterns of giving or even of missionary service may be motivated by subterranean feelings of guilt. Economists talk about high income countries and low income countries. We are aware, if we want to be, that the gap between the two is already massive and growing larger. We also know that within the poor nations there are substantial numbers of people with no income. It is true that we may be genuinely confused as to the historical and current reasons for this discrepancy, and what kinds of solution ought to be attempted so that all may have a decent standard of living. But as Christians we fully understand the obligation to be generous. So, we give what we think we can afford from our disposable income (after we have been reasonably generous to ourselves and our families) to help those in need.

Charitable giving has always been closely associated with religious commitment, either as a means of salvation or a response to salvation. It has been extolled by the modern advocates of free-market economics as a responsible and personal way of redistributing wealth. However, it does not necessarily correspond to the economic realities of the living poor, doing little or nothing over the long term to give them proper opportunities to work, earn and live in dignity. The issue of truth, in this case that of justice, may be further obscured by the emotional relief of knowing that we are not wholly selfish with what we have received. Thus, what in other circumstances would be considered a highly commendable act of unselfishness may sadly become a hindrance to a real, long-term solution to a very grave and stubborn crisis of structural poverty.

RELIGION, HANDMAID OF CIVIL SOCIETY

Those who do not think that, on balance, religion is of some benefit to society are few. Attempts to create a brave new world of moral rectitude based on other than religious convictions have not inspired many followers.

In the nature of the case many of them are anti-authoritarian, based on the premise that religions impose arbitrary restrictions on freedom. As a result, they tend strongly towards a libertarian interpretation of conduct. As in so many other fields, criticism of the prevailing moral climate does not automatically provide a better alternative. Libertarianism runs into the problem of boundaries. The frontiers of the moral life are so open that anything is allowed to pass. The only criterion of judgement is personal taste. Individuals, then, are the whole government in their respective territories. They alone have the authority to decide what should happen. Needless to say, there is no opposition party!

Allowing the individual totalitarian rights over their own lives would be the only alternative on an otherwise uninhabited desert island. In a crowded and highly diversified society the individual has to fit into a social community where the opinions, rights and responsibilities of others also count. Hence, a society, to function as more than the sum total of individual beliefs and aspirations, has to try to engender a moral consensus.

Religion, as probably the greatest generator of culture, is usually turned to as the basis for this consensus. Agreement can only come on the basis of past values and traditions, which in most societies have their origin in a view of life above and beyond the flux of everyday circumstances, a stable reference-point to which all can turn. Even where values are changing, as they are doing at a steady rate in secularised societies, religion is looked to as the agent to manage change. Thus, for example, where the consensus is for considerable freedom of sexual activity, the Christian virtues of tolerance and a non-judgemental attitude are extolled.

Religion is used as an instrument to avoid the breakdown of that imperceptible and inevitably fragile consent, or at least passive acquiescence, which allows societies to be relatively free of violent agitation. Its role in civil society is definitely not seen as one of challenge and opposition. Prophets may be all right in another age or a different part of the world. They are clearly not welcome at home (as Jesus Christ himself found).

Nationalist aspirations have often laid hold of religious traditions to motivate a people to demand changes: Protestants and Catholics in Northern Ieland, Jews settling on the West Bank territory of Palestine, Iranians in the overthrow of the Pahlavi dynasty, Sinhalese in Sri Lanka, the Rashtriya Swayum Sang in India, and many ethnic groups in Eastern Europe and the Soviet Union in recent years.

Nowhere, perhaps, is the place and importance of religion more clearly, and tragically, seen than in the legitimation of violence and war. Both because of its deep roots in the consciousness of a people and because of its tendency to dogmatic certainties, religion can easily be persuaded to endorse the collective need, in certain circumstances, for an enemy. Much easier if that enemy is perceived to belong to another religion. 'Love your enemies, do good to those who hate you' is a counsel of despair for religion.

RELIGION, THE ETERNAL RETURN

Some critics of religion, most notably Marxists, have analysed the phenomenon of religion in terms of its function in society. They see it as part of the established order, having the task of policing the populace so that it may not become conscious of injustices and discrimination and demand the overthrow of the privileged. Thus, for example, there has been in recent years an enormous amount of effort spent in trying to demonstrate that Christianity is not hostile to the accumulation of wealth. Those Christians who would identify politically with the conservative 'new right' adopt the subtle posture of accusing socialist-inclined Christians of being opposed to wealth creation. They then demonstrate biblically and historically that wealth creation was intended by God as a means of enjoying the bounty of his creation. The deduction from this line of reasoning is that the economic system which has shown itself in practice to be the most accomplished in creating wealth should be supported. Christians, therefore, ought not to oppose free-market capitalism. At most, they may question some of its more unfortunate consequences.

This is one example, albeit an important one, of the way in which religion may be co-opted to prevent substantial change in the way things are. Another might be the issue of racism. It is easy for Christians to dismiss the reality of racist attitudes and practices within the Church with the glib assertion that, of course, Christianity does not tolerate them. The need for change is rejected by a facile use of texts like Galatians 3:28 and Colossians 3:11, divorced from sensitivity to what is actually happening between communities.

If and when people of strong religious beliefs do challenge the basic assumptions on which economies or laws are based, they are told that religion (or religious leaders) has no competence to pronounce on political matters. It is a 'heads I win, tails you lose' situation: if religion can be managed in such a way that it approves the given order, it is to be honoured and advocated; if it turns critical, it is to be marginalised.

It is notorious how religion has played a major role in allowing people to escape from the apparently ceaseless change of ordinary life into a realm of permanence and certainty. Eastern religions start from the premise that physical existence is inferior and that the multiplicity of experience must give way to a consciousness of the unity of everything. Salvation is achieved in the final escape from the ceaseless round of rebirths into this world.

Christianity, as we have already mentioned, has been profoundly influenced by the divorce between spiritual and material reality inherited from the classical period of Greek philosophical thought. The ideal world is beyond change. Heaven beckons. Spiritual growth is most perfectly achieved by renouncing the pleasures of this life. The journey to eternal bliss is best made by journeying away from current civilisation into the desert or into the sanctuary of the silent monastic order.

Even for those who have committed themselves to marriage, family and work, where physical withdrawal is not an option, there are plenty of other means of escape. One might be the flight from reason, in which intellectual thought about the meaning and application of the faith is considered a distraction from spiritual life. Another might be the search for spiritual experiences, in which the goal is release from the tensions and traumas of ordinary life. Yet another might be the expectation that the reality of heaven can be reproduced here and now in physical healing and relief from pain. It is a salutary comment on the state of Christianity when all these happenings are considered to be signs of spiritual renewal. If they remain the absorbing interests of Christians, then the faith has been converted into religion. The line from one to the other can easily be crossed while hardly realising what has happened.

The subversion of Christianity

The conclusion of our discussion so far is that the original gospel message of Jesus Christ and the apostles has been converted in countless ways into the essence of religion. Fortunately, the possibility of real reformation has always been present. In spite of the pressures of culture and political regimes, the Church does not have to put itself uncritically at the disposal of the most powerful interest groups of the moment. It is precisely because faith and religion are not to be identified that reform and change become possible. In the next chapter we will look more closely at some of the ways in which the Christian faith as practised might change. At this stage we need to clarify the theological distinctions which enable the recovery of true discipleship to take place. I will briefly discuss the three principal ones.

FROM THE KINGDOM OF GOD TO THE KINGDOMS OF THIS WORLD

At the very centre of what Jesus said and did is the kingdom of God. It is the good news from God which he proclaimed in Galilee, after John had been imprisoned (Mk. 1:14–15), and which he demonstrated when John, in prison, sent disciples to ask whether he was the long-expected Messiah (Mt. 11:2–6).

The kingdom is God's final and complete salvation, when the righteous will be vindicated, those who oppose God judged, justice established among the nations, and a new created order of welfare for all inaugurated. It is human life in full recognition of God's rule. Everything in the created order will express restoration to the perfection which God both demands and offers.

It is not only a hope for the future but also God's power at work now, making a new way of being human a reality in the present. For this reason, it also represents a summons to a new style of life. In their personal lives and in society all are called to restore wholeness to human life by overcoming disease, mental distress, prejudice and violence, and by creating a situation in which all may participate freely in the fruits of wealth.

The kingdom of God is thus a divine project in which human beings are called, through the one perfect representative of the kingdom, to collaborate with God. However, in numerous ways, it has been converted into a human project in which God is called upon to collaborate with us. 'Render to Caesar what is Caesar's' has either taken precedence over 'render to God . . . ', or has been totally separated from it, so that particular social and political programmes have become identified with the will of God.

This is a subtle process in which highly commendable goals, like the maximisation of individual talents or the provision of secondary education for all, are abstracted from a whole way of life and set of values and made the touchstone of correct Christian commitment and practice. In theological terms, the coming kingdom is reduced, under pressure of the immediate situation, to one of its component parts. We seek to squeeze the wide contours of God's future salvation into the narrow valley of our limited vision. As a result the kingdom becomes domesticated and trivialised. It is re-created as a religious adjunct to a cramped human political programme.

FROM A PILGRIM PEOPLE TO THE ARK OF SALVATION

One of the finest definitions of the Church, probably inspired by the Epistle to the Hebrews, is Helder Camara's picture of it as 'the Abrahamic community'. Like the father of the Hebrew people, it is always being called to leave where it is and move on. It is symbolised by a tent, a functional but impermanent provision for the journey. It can be easily packed up, carried and pitched in some new place as one travels to the chosen destination. Travellers are not, then, absorbed by the time and problems of maintaining a permanent set of buildings, only the relatively uncomplicated task of striking camp when necessary. The journey itself and the final goal absorb most of the necessary energies.

Contrast with this the image of the Church as an ark. This model sees the Church as a safe haven from the dangerous storms of a hostile world, a place to escape to from the wrath to come. It is essentially a refuge of warmth and security as it sails towards the life to come. The primary mission of the Church is to rescue people from drowning in the floods of scepticism and moral anarchy.

The ark, of course, is a very solid building. To do its job it needs plenty of maintenance. The main preoccupations of the crew will be to make sure that the vessel is in pristine order and always heading in the right direction. Much time will be given to looking after the boat itself, with a little time to rescue shipwrecked casualties, as long as they are close enough.

Moreover, it is vital to the efficiency of the operation that there be no mutiny on board. The commands of the captain and his immediate subordinates must be obeyed at all times. There cannot be any serious dispute about the direction of the ship, or it would finish up going round in circles. Those who run the boat are the professional seafarers, the ones who have spent most time in it and, literally, know the ropes.

FROM RESURRECTION TO IMMORTALITY

The following quotation from Jon Sobrino sums up another catastrophic shift which the early Church made from faith to religion:

> No longer did the liturgy express the eschatological consciousness of the community as an assembly in which the Spirit was present to guarantee salvation. Instead the celebration of the Lord's supper was viewed as a medicinal remedy guaranteeing immortality. Salvation of the individual and homage to the risen Lord began to swallow up the life of discipleship in obedience to the crucified Jesus, which seeks to be a transforming presence in the world in anticipation of the making of all things new. (Sobrino 1985:191)

The point that Sobrino is making here is that the Christian liturgy's primary aim is the strengthening and renewing of the Christian community for costly service in the world, not the pure contemplation of an abstract God. Christian salvation is resurrection from the dead in order that by word and deed the saved may bear witness to the source of all life here and now in the midst of corruption and decay. It is not the flight of the soul from mortality to the eternal.

Thus, the worship of God is carried on in the world, not apart from it. It is not designed to free us from the distractions of life, but to give us the right perspective upon them. In many ways it would be more fittingly carried out on a ploughed field, at an assembly line or in an office than in a church or chapel building. The Muslim or Christian group – I have seen both – praying openly in the concourse of an airport is much more appropriate than retiring to the chapel sometimes provided.

Jesus Christ died outside the gate

Whatever the precise division of responsibility for Jesus' death, it is of the essence of the witness of the New Testament that he was crucified for directly challenging the power of the religious establishment and indirectly threatening the established divine–human order of Rome. The cross of Jesus is much more than a symbol. It is the inevitable, historical consequence of one who mediated God's judgement on religion as a means for gaining and administering power.

The author of Hebrews statement that Jesus was put to death outside the gate of the holy city Jerusalem is the climax of a long argument in which he affirms that whoever follows Jesus has no need of any other religious performance. He himself is the prophet like Moses and the priest like Melchizedek. He is an apostle like Joshua. He is the altar and sacrifice, and the way through the curtain into God's presence. He is the one who strengthens and perfects our faith, and brings us finally to the heavenly Jerusalem, the city of the living God, the kingdom which cannot be shaken.

He not only fulfilled the law and all the ritual requirements of religion, but showed them to be insubstantial, shadows of the good things that were coming. They were not ultimately real at all, and therefore in the light of the coming of the true reality they became valueless (Heb. 13:9).

These are judgements which religion cannot tolerate, for it represents an immense amount of intellectual labour, spiritual sacrifice and moral endeavour – often of breath-taking ability and quality. And yet, as a way of solving the profound problems of human life which it has arisen to resolve, it is worthless. No wonder Jesus had to be sacrificed in order that the temple and the nation might be preserved (Jn. 11:50). The straw that broke the camel's back was Jesus' claim, in the context of the cleansing of the temple, that his body would replace the holy place as the way to the Father (Jn. 2:19–22).

It was absolutely logical that Jesus would be judicially murdered in the place where the remains of the sacrifices were thrown. The symbolic force of this historical fact is immense: as F. F. Bruce (1964:402) says, 'Jesus was led outside Jerusalem to be crucified, and this is regarded as a token of his rejection by all that Jerusalem represented.' Religion threw him away, just as the carcasses of the animals were discarded and burned.

This being so, Jesus' disciples are to be where he is: outside religion (i.e., outside those cumulative beliefs, rituals and traditions of a community which not only do not have the power to free people to enjoy a restored relationship to God, their creator and sustainer, but may actively prevent it). There, with him, they will expect to bear the full consequences of their action of deliberately excluding themselves from the religious and national community – it is a disgrace (Heb. 13:13). This stepping outside is a picture of conversion. It is supremely important, however, that the author of Hebrews does not represent this as leaving one religion and joining another, even less of discarding an inferior faith in order to embrace a superior one. It is a conversion from every form of religious commitment, to Jesus, who, in the words of another apostle (Rom. 10:4), is the end of the law (that is, every conceivable means of securing God's pleasure).

This whole discussion leads to the necessary conclusion that the faith which has at its centre the Jesus of the New Testament cannot be compared with either the systems of belief or the rites and practices of what are generally acknowledged to be the religions of the world. In order to try to find parallels, people are forced to do one of two things: either to point to peripheral similarities, but leaving the heart of the matter untouched, or to convert or reduce faith in Jesus to the mere 'religion' of Christianity. If and when another faith is discovered which centres its whole hope for a transformed human existence on a crucified God, there will be plenty of room for discussion.

7

Freedom from Christianity

'If the advocates of prudence and patience were to take a trip around the world, they'd get an enormous shock. You can't regulate the Holy Spirit.'

—**Helder Camara**

'The message made flesh in the life of the Church gives to it the solid platform from which to proclaim the Gospel of the Kingdom. Such an actualisation helps to restore fully to the Church its true missionary character.'

—**Ken Gnanakan**

'What does an alternative movement do when it is successful? . . . The tendency of the . . . institutional Church is to assimilate itself to the existing power and to be tamed by it rather than taming it.'

—**Ulrich Duchrow and Gerhard Liedke**

Paradoxically, one of the greatest strengths of Christian faith is its ability to deal creatively and confidently with abject failures. In principle, at least, those who seek to live after the pattern of Jesus Christ have no need for pretence. They are free to admit mistakes and absurdities. There is no particular reason, apart from a normal human tendency in this direction, why they should need to justify the error of their ways. Never are Christians more faithful to the message they say they believe than when they admit their frequent faults.

The end of law

The reason for this is found in one of the great central affirmations of belief: 'The law was given through Moses; grace and truth came through Jesus Christ' (Jn. 1:17). In this statement we come close to the heart of the difference between religion and real faith. Law (that is, right or appropriate conduct) is at the heart of every religion. In its original context the law referred to the detailed prescriptions for living in community that God gave to his people through the great prophet and leader Moses. God (the one Lord), the law, Moses and the people were fundamental elements of Jewish faith. One might, without too much distortion, exchange Moses for Muhammad in order to find the substance of Islam: the Qur'an contains detailed prescriptions for living in community which Allah (there is no other Lord) revealed to the world through the great prophet and leader Muhammad. With somewhat less credibility, perhaps, we could delete Moses to find the basis for common Hindu practice, and for Buddhism delete Moses and God. What is common in each case is the fundamental centrality of law for the correct interpretation and practice of religion.

It would be necessary, of course, to insist that law is being used here in a very wide sense. For it to be one of the central affirmations of all religions, we would need to understand it in terms of the great variety of obligations necessary to achieve the respective goal of each religion.

When we come to the main story of the New Testament and its interpretation, however, we are breathing a wholly different atmosphere. It is not that God's law is put on one side or treated with disrespect, for there are plenty of passages which speak of the fulfilment of the law. It is rather that the law is placed in a new context, that of the coming of Jesus Christ into the world. According to John's Gospel, the law *was given* through Moses. The passive tense must be a truism for any monotheistic religion. God alone is the source and revealer of right and wrong action. What is unusual and different is the claim that Jesus Christ *brought with him* grace and truth. From now on the essence of faith is determined by the meaning of grace and truth, as demonstrated in the life of Jesus, rather than by law.

It is in understanding this that one can appreciate why Christian faith proclaims that recognition of failure and error is the beginning of good news. Truth refers to the reality of who God is, who we are, and what is the true interpretation of our situation in the world. According to the story of Jesus, God is perfect in all his actions, totally consistent in his love and justice. He is, to use an exclusively biblical word, a holy God. Holiness is a robust word, whose meaning can only be partially captured by words like purity, truthfulness, faithfulness, goodness and generosity. These attributes of God's character are, naturally, stamped on the universe which he has created. The human world in particular is made to function according to the holiness or truth of God.

Holiness cannot be captured in the regulations of laws. Laws can only approximate to the requirements of a holy life. It is possible, as Saul the Pharisee claimed in all sincerity, to keep fully the precepts of the law. It may not be easy. One may have to decide to dedicate one's life almost exclusively to the pursuit of the righteousness which the law demands. But with rigour of devotion and abstinence from otherwise legitimate pursuits it is possible to obey the law.

However, when Paul the apostle had seen the blinding light of God's holiness in the face of Jesus Christ on the Damascus road, he knew that following the law was a totally inadequate way of meeting God as he really is. What is hard for human beings as they are is to have a deep inner desire, above all else, to be like God. Religion tends to content itself with observance of the regulations; true faith goes much deeper, to the inner meaning and purpose of the law.

As Jesus told in his brilliant story about the religious

leader and the religious failure (Lk. 18:9–14; cf. also Jn. 1:16; Rom. 5:15–21; 2 Cor. 8:9; Eph. 2:5–8), God has supplied another way, that of grace. The story is extremely subtle and sets a trap for the unwary. It is easy to think that Jesus is so right to condemn this self-satisfied, self-righteous attender at the temple. It is the mistake that many make when they judge church-goers to be hypocrites. Just as we give three cheers for the sinner and condemn the nasty, conceited Pharisee, we condemn ourselves.

The confession of the sinner was utterly sincere. It was wholly transparent, nothing was hidden, no excuses were made. He had no other motive for approaching God than deep sorrow for a rotten and selfish life. He might have said, 'God, I am a terrible sinner, I have done awful things with my life, but at least I am not like this arrogant Pharisee.' But he did not compare himself with anyone else, only with God's holiness. He then cast himself entirely on God's mercy and on God's desire to forgive, reconcile and restore. This is God's grace! And grace, as the story so powerfully proclaims, cuts across the noblest and most admirable religion in the world.

The law – just and compassionate action in all circumstances – is part of true faith, but it follows grace. It is not abrogated, but it is made possible by the new relationship which God has established between himself and us through Jesus Christ. The law by itself, as a naked command to obey, brings a terrible burden. Anyone who really means business with the law should despair of ever being able to atone for their failures. Hence, wherever law in its myriad forms remains the driving force of people's beliefs and practices, there we have evidence of religion at work. Wherever there is a glimpse of the true meaning of grace, there we are on the threshold of a breakthrough to a different plane of reality.

Means of escape

Christianity, in spite of its foundational texts, has often been converted into another religion. It has fallen back from its calling to live by grace and for grace. There are a number of ways in which this has come about. Most prominent is the conversion of true faith into institutional formalism in which projects and programmes take over as the guiding force of the community's life. This could be characterised as a form of escapism from the kind of discipleship centred on truth and grace.

One form of escapism is the variety of evangelistic programmes which abound in the Church today. The intention is undoubtedly excellent. There is a right desire to tell others about the story of Jesus in such a way that they too become followers and live by truth and grace. However, in many church circles, particularly evangelical ones, today's strategies for reaching 'the unreached' have come to dominate thinking and action in regard to evangelisation.

Some are advocating the fulfilment of the quite meaningless slogan, 'The evangelisation of the world by the year 2000.' This is interpreted as the presence of Christian communities in every major 'people group' by the end of the millennium. Is the penetration of every distinct ethnic group by Christians from outside in order to plant churches among them the same as evangelisation? How can one possibly tie down the Holy Spirit's work to the year 2000? If that is the definition and the strategy, then it will fail. Many human communities will continue to remain largely impervious to that kind of missionary endeavour.

The re-evangelisation of previously 'Christianised' nations is also highly problematical. This is not because people do not desperately need to hear, believe and practise the message of grace and truth as it is in Jesus, but because evangelism is so often related to membership of existing church bodies. In spite of the many theological and statistical doubts about 'mass evangelism', there remain many church leaders who continue to advocate it as one major way of reaching the population with the gospel. The transformation of individual lives through a personal encounter with the living Jesus Christ is clearly the object of the exercise. The means used, however, are the somewhat stylised preaching of a message, the call to go forward, the registering of people's names, addresses and levels of commitment, and the encouragement of a local church to incorporate them into its life and activities. Is that true evangelisation? Is it not rather an escape into a counterfeit appearance of it?

Another form of escapism is social activism. Many Christians are inclined to interpret their calling wholly in terms of the struggle to enable suffering and marginalised people to liberate themselves from the injustices of their situation. It is becoming fashionable, particularly among some in Asia, to replace the idea of the mission of the Church and the mission of Christ with that of the *missio Dei*. Thus, the Korean theologian Kim Yong-Bock (1990:7) says:

> the ecumenical movement in Asia has undergone a shift from the ecclesio-centric paradigm of Western Christendom to the people-centred paradigm, with which the Gospel is intertwined . . . The theology of Missio Dei has greatly influenced Christian communities' participation in society, since the traditional notion of the mission of the Church was too limiting . . . The mission of the Church was preoccupied with evangelistic and social service concerns.

The theological conviction underlying this shift is quite simple:

> The most basic theological affirmation is that the peoples of Asia are the children of God . . . The dalits, janata, minjung, the poor, oppressed, women and the ethnically and culturally alienated in Asia are the very people of God. The Mission of God among the suffering people of Asia is to restore their life and dignity to the fullest. (12)

The work of the Christian Church, then, is to identify itself with those who are already God's people in order to be a means of bringing among them both liberation from *han* (a deep sense of being wronged) and freedom.

Kim Yong-Bock is quite explicit in pointing to the causes of the people's indignity:

> God makes the poor socio-economically secure; God frees and liberates those oppressed and imprisoned by the dictatorial powers. God establishes justice, overthrowing the structures and systems of injustice. God gives peace to the refugees, the exiled people, the captives in the desolate, war-torn wastelands. (12)

Is this the heart and substance of the truth and grace of Jesus Christ? Here there is no recognition that the people themselves may be in part the cause of their own indignity. No sin, only being sinned against. No humble desire for forgiveness, only the demand for rights and justice.

In one highly significant sentence, Kim Yong-Bock summarises his vision of the goal of liberation: 'God's work among the suffering people in Asia is the establishment of God's Sovereign Rule of justice, in which the people become sovereign' (13). So, the work of Christ is seen not as liberation from the corruption of power, by whomever exercised and at whatever level, but simply the exchange of power. This vision can only spring from a naive and romantic view of those who today are the oppressed peoples. Implicitly it undermines the need for truth and grace as set forth in the life, death and resurrection of Jesus, the Christ. The sinner, after all, is more righteous than the Pharisee.

A third form of escapsim is renewal. Like evangelisation and social involvement, this is a necessary part of Christian life and witness. Indeed, it might well be considered a prerequisite for the other two. Renewal means to wake up from a state of great drowsiness. It is like a purposeful and invigorating walk in the strong wind of the Spirit. Renewal also means to make something useful out of a failure, as sometimes has to happen when the most careful cooking goes wrong!

The renewal of the Church, therefore, ought to mean

rousing God's people from a soporific state of inaction and indecision, strengthening what life remains, changing its shape where it is ineffective, and bringing hope where there may be despair. How, then, is it possible for renewal to be a means of escape from the true following of Jesus Christ? The answer is by hijacking the concept and restricting its application to only certain aspects of the Church's life.

Like other buzz words (radical, liberation, the poor, the people, partnership) renewal is no one's monopoly. Sadly, however, this is what it has become. When some people speak about a person, group or community being open to renewal they usually mean that they are wanting to manifest the gifts of the Spirit in their corporate or individual life, to see healings take place by the direct action of God, to be involved in personal counselling and a ministry of deliverance from evil powers and to have an open style of worship in which prophecy, words of knowledge and revelation are spoken, and people are free to praise God in tongues and dance as the Spirit leads them.

These are highly desirable demonstrations of the goodness and power of God in the midst of his people, bringing them further into a right relationship with himself and with one another. But, are they the sum total of renewal? Renewal is not a common word in the New Testament, though other words with similar meanings are used. In fact, it occurs in only three contexts: the renewal of our inner being (2 Cor. 4:16), the renewal of our minds (Rom. 12:2; Col. 3:10) and renewal in repentance (Heb. 6:6). The global statement, 'He saved us through the washing of rebirth and renewal by the Holy Spirit' (Tit. 3:5), may be considered to cover all three. However, using other words, Jesus in one passage speaks of the renewal (or rebirth) of all things (Mt. 19:28), the apostle Paul of the redemption of creation (Rom. 8:21) and the elder John of the new heavens and the new earth (Rev. 21:1).

It is fair to ask, when the idea of renewal is being discussed: Are all these dimensions being included? Unfortunately, I fear not. Renewal means 'going on to maturity', that is fully facing all the responsibilities inherent in following Jesus Christ, full of grace and truth. It means leaving behind one's spiritual, emotional and intellectual childhood in a process of growth into the full likeness of Jesus Christ.

An indispensable part of this growth is the transformation of the way we think. In the context of a passage which deals extensively with the gifts of prophecy and speaking in tongues, Paul tells the Corinthian Christians sharply, 'stop thinking like children . . . in your thinking be adults' (1 Cor. 14:20). In the midst of extensive spiritual manifestations, they displayed evidence of considerable immaturity. In spite of this injunction, however, in modern movements of renewal this aspect usually receives scant attention. Indeed, some people, claiming to be renewed in the Spirit, consciously view intellectual activity as a dangerous threat to spiritual vitality. Even though this perspective may be extreme, it would probably strike us as strange to hear someone praying that our minds might be renewed in order that our spiritual lives might be strengthened.

Paul's opinion is quite categorical. There is no renewal that leaves the mind untouched. The mind determines whether we are going to be conformed to the present state of the world, under judgement and passing away, or be transformed to live according to new life in Christ. The mind determines whether our Christian commitment is weak and confused or vigorous and purposeful.

In some circles the search for renewal appears to be a social phenomenon: people needing relief from the suffocating materialism, scepticism and anonymity of the highly pressurised existence of advanced industrialised societies. The high expectation of physical and emotional healing may have something to do with modern society's belief that technological expertise can put right whatever does not function properly. It is not often that people in the renewal movement are prominent in calling for just dealings within the international community. Sometimes one gets the impression that Christians believe that fundamental change is impossible within the sphere of business, political life, education, the law, the media, and so on. Genuine freedom is only possible in the life of the Spirit in the sphere of the Church.

The basic problem with all these forms of escapism is that policies and procedures have converted the amazing story of the grace and truth of Jesus Christ into a dwarf gospel. Planned activities have taken the place of that new life in the Spirit of Christ which should issue in a lifestyle of solidarity with all vulnerable people, resistance to all manifestations of corrupt power, a commending of the liberating power of the grace of Jesus, a transformed way of thinking, and growth into spiritual maturity. Only when all these aspects of Christian faith are present can one say that religion has been overcome.

The Church, old and new

The typical local church in many parts of the world represents Christianity as a religious phenomenon. But there are also new visions for the Church, pregnant with hope and opportunity.

In the first case, we see churches, often quite unconsciously, geared to survival. Much of their activity is centred on the buildings, although the church itself may only be used on Sundays, and perhaps occasionally during the week. The major effort of the leadership seems to be to maintain a fairly fixed programme of activities. This may vary slightly from year to year and from minister to minister, but usually within well-defined boundaries.

To an outsider such a church would appear to be organising itself for its own members, with the occasional recruitment drive outside. It has effectively been squeezed into the mould of a voluntary club, with rules and regulations, a well-defined membership, and activities to meet the expectations of its most dedicated patrons. Nevertheless, it differs radically from most clubs and interest groups in that its activities do not actually match up to its declared aims and objectives.

One of the main problems is the inertia of the institution. Many Christians simply accept unthinkingly the traditional activities of the church as constituting its life and purpose. The church is defined by what it does, and what it does by the pattern of events inherited from the past. Yet, if it desires to be more than just another religious institution, to be a genuine community of disciples of the one who came among us full of grace and truth, it needs to convert itself from one way of looking at its life to another.

The church does not consist in the abundance of the things which it does, particularly when these are behind the walls of its own premises. Its calling is effectively fulfilled when it gives itself in service to those outside and challenges them to surrender to the righteous rule of God, their creator and saviour.

Christians live in the world. Mission, therefore, is not being sent into the world from outside it, but moving from one part of the world to another (even within the same locality).

Christians, unfortunately, are often guilty of trying to relate the gospel to abstract human essences – disembodied spirits, beyond the boundaries of the Church, that need to be saved. But people are complex beings in which emotions, mind and body interact in many extraordinary ways. If we are to love them with the same kind of love that God has displayed towards us, we must relate to them as they are. Love is not a vague emotion, but commitment to real people in a web of relationships in the midst of very concrete circumstances. In the life of Christ this is sensitively illustrated in the case of the Samaritan woman at Jacob's well (Jn. 4:1–26).

If the Church is gradually going to be converted to a new way of being, there are a number of obstacles to overcome, or tendencies to resist. One is *institutionalisation* which manifests itself in an unwillingness to allow organisations to cease. Because they have always been there, they must be kept going at all costs. If new forms of church life were to be put into operation, many fear there would be a further decline in membership. And yet, with very few exceptions, many organisations (particularly those for young people) are not effective at either keeping people in the Christian community or enlisting new members.

A second obstacle is *ritualism*. Patterns of worship are repeated from the past because they are familiar and the members are accustomed to them. Worship too often seems to be orientated around the two syndromes of withdrawal and security. The language used, the means of communication adopted, the musical instruments considered appropriate, the way the building is furnished and laid out, all seem designed to distance the Christian community that meets there once a week from the ordinary, everyday life of society. The unspoken fallacy at the heart of much worship is the belief that sacredness is the opposite of the secular.

In the many debates about worship, one assumption which is often forcibly expressed is that it must have a timeless quality. Change is said to detract from the human being's approach to the majesty of God. There are two further, hidden fallacies underlying this strong conviction. Firstly, that we come into God's presence by moving from the constant ebb and flow of our time-bound existence into the timeless stillness of eternity. Secondly, that 'timelessness' requires adherence to the past. This cannot be so, for if, to take an example, the arguments used for maintaining seventeenth-century language in the liturgy and biblical text had been applied in the seventeenth century, we would presumably now still be using the language of Chaucer!

Worship ought to be a special time the community sets apart, when together its members can meet with God in the midst of their various activities and responsibilities in the world. Sadly, it is often seen as a time of coming apart, when the world can be kept at a safe distance. It is then debased into a means of assurance against the confusion of the present and the threat of the future. Whereas the only real assurance the Christian has is to be in step with Jesus Christ, the Pioneer and Perfecter of our faith.

The third and perhaps most serious obstacle is that of *professionalism*. There can be little doubt that, whatever is said about the priesthood of all believers, or whatever may be the current rhetoric about every-member ministry, in practice the life of the local church revolves around the abilities, gifts, expectations and vision (or lack of these qualities) of the ordained minister. This causes a grave problem for the church, for its mission can only proceed at the pace and in the direction which the official leader is willing to allow or is able to cope with.

I have spoken to many ministers in local churches, almost all of whom display a fear of allowing ministry to develop as the Spirit equips and Jesus Christ sends. They seem to interpret their calling to mean control rather than release. They collude with the congregation's traditional expectation that the minister is appointed to co-ordinate, if not actually do the work of ministry. This seems so obvious. What other possible function could the minister have?

Well, let us suppose that a different model of the Church from the current one operated. It would consist primarily of small fellowships of people committed to practising and speaking about the grace and truth of Jesus Christ in all kinds of ordinary situations in society. It would have moved away from the notion of the local church as an institution with set obligations and activities to perform. According to this model, the ordained minister would not have much of an institution to run and maintain. She or he would be free to facilitate the communities in their missionary calling, where they are and where God calls them to go. The ordained minister would have a key role to play, not in deciding what the fellowship should be doing, but in assessing the involvement of its members and encouraging and enabling them to be more faithful.

As is well known by now, such communities of believers are emerging in different parts of the world, including Europe. They do not conform to a set pattern, but in so far as they are genuinely trying to 'reinvent the Church' (the subtitle of Leonardo Boff's book, *Ecclesiogenesis*) they have certain characteristics. The following are a few of them.

Firstly, the leadership emerges from within the community itself, according to the gifts given to each. There may be a single leader or group leadership. In either case it seeks a genuine participation of the whole community in decision-making processes.

Secondly, the ordained leadership of the church is seen as a vital resource for the life and witness of the community and a link with the wider community of communities.

Thirdly, the communities do not seek to grow too large. Rather than expand their own number, they would prefer to bring into being other, non-dependent groups.

Fourthly, they meet wherever is convenient. It may be a home, or a local community building such as a school or day-care centre, or a church. They are free from concern for the maintenance of the plant.

Fifthly, their Christian witness is orientated towards what is happening within the wider human community of which they are part. Their evangelisation arises out of the presence of the members within different local organisations and the service they seek to offer to their neighbourhood.

Sixthly, when they meet together it is to pray, give thanks to God and study the Bible in the light of their experiences during the week.

Here, it would seem, we have a model for other Christians to emulate. Of course, the Christian community is by no means perfect. It often struggles with the perennial problems of human relationships. Nevertheless, it suggests a way in which the Christian faith is being concretely lived out in communities of believers free of religious preoccupation.

In the final chapter I will try to explore why and how Jesus Christ is the fullness of liberation from the chains of religion. Before that, I would like to present a historical case study from the Acts of the Apostles of how the first churches dealt with the challenge of a pluralist culture.

8

Coming to Terms with Pluralism: A Study of the Early Church

'Mission to the Jews is the oldest Christian mission; that's where it all began . . . Either all people need Christ or none do!'
—**Gerald Anderson**

'The first century was a period marked by pluralism. The collapse of confidence in the classical gods of Greece and Rome had left a cavernous vacuum, and into it flowed every imaginable kind of popular philosophy, esoteric cult and mystery religion.'
—**Os Guinness**

From the periphery to the centre

The first Christians took the message of Jesus to people who followed many different religious beliefs. They found themselves in a situation not unlike our own, in which people enjoyed considerable freedom to find and practise a religion which they believed best suited their needs.

A plurality of freely available religious beliefs and practices is not just a recent phenomenon with which the Church, for the first time in its history, has to come to terms. Sometimes Christians who are engaged in dialogue with people of other faiths give the impression that Christianity's tendency to stress its exclusive nature is due to the fact that it has always been a dominant religion. The fact that the modern missionary movement arose at a time of Western economic and political expansion has been given as a reason for either rejecting or being extremely cautious about a missionary approach to people of other religious traditions.

However, this is only one side of the equation. There was absolutely nothing imperialist (in the political sense) about the missionary movement of the first three centuries. Indeed, to use modern categories, the early Christians moved in their missionary work from the periphery (an obscure province on the eastern edge of the Roman Empire) to the centre, the capital city of a vast empire. Whatever the motivation of more recent missionary efforts by the churches, that of the earliest Christians could never have been seen as a justification of territorial aggrandisement.

This being so, though historically important for the way in which relationships between Christianity and other faiths have developed in recent centuries, the relationship between Western colonialism and evangelism is ultimately irrelevant. The early Church, at least (and one must include the churches of the East for most of their history), did not seek to justify its evangelistic work on the grounds that it was spreading a better civilisation. This is equally true today of the emerging missions of the Third World Church which, following the pattern of the earliest period, are once again moving from the periphery to the centre.

Therefore, it is a historical anachronism to make the Western experience of the last few centuries into a negative paradigm which should lead us to convert mission into dialogue and coexistence. True, the Church has many sobering lessons to learn from this experience. It is more important, however, to go back to the beginning to explore why and how the first Christians engaged in evangelism in a multi-religious, multi-cultural, pluralist world.

This is the intention of this chapter. Naturally, it cannot attempt anything like a comprehensive survey of a complex situation. Instead it will focus on one presentation of the story – that by Luke in the second part of the Book of Acts – confident that this gives us a faithful account of the way the early Church came to terms with the plurality of beliefs of its own world. For Christians in the twentieth century this should ultimately be a more relevant paradigm than the situation which may have prevailed in more recent times.

Is the story history?

By adopting this approach, we are not, however, free of problems. Some interpreters of the New Testament believe that a strong apologetic motive in writing history makes that history suspect. So in this case Luke, the travelling companion of Paul, was bound to have presented the details of the history he wrote in such a way as to have distorted at least some of the events he describes. Add to this the belief of a few scholars that the author of Acts (not Luke at all) lived some fifty or so years after the events he records, and therefore could not have had accurate information about them.

It is beyond the scope of this study to discuss these matters in any great depth. Being aware of the debate, I would, however, like to offer some response to the sceptical attitudes which some scholars have adopted.

In the first place, I accept the need for a critical approach to all historical writing. This means that one does not necessarily take what the author says at face value. It is important to investigate the purposes for which he wrote, the context in which he found himself, and the sources he may have used. In judging historical reliability one should not dismiss out of hand the possibility that the author has consciously or unconsciously allowed his particular bias to distort his presentation of some of the events. At the same time, starting from the premise that the author *must* have allowed his stance to affect his accuracy negatively is no more sound than to begin the other way round. Indeed, it is commonly accepted that according to the principle of natural justice a person is innocent until proved, beyond all reasonable doubt, to be guilty.

There is no reason, therefore, why we should not accept that Luke is telling the story as it happened, unless and until there is conclusive evidence that distortions have crept in. In other words, the burden of proof is on those who believe he may be inaccurate. It is not good enough for them to be suspicious. They must be able to demonstrate that Luke in fact presents his facts in such a way that either they are internally inconsistent or else they contradict other facts of which there can be no doubt.

Suffice it to say that at this stage of our knowledge Luke's own claim to have investigated every element of the story carefully, in order to confirm its accuracy (Lk. 1:1–4), has generally been vindicated. Most of the doubts about the circumstances he describes have been dispelled. In one of the most recent studies (Hemer 1989), Luke's historical accuracy is continually confirmed.

We repeat that theories which reconstruct what might or must have happened are worthless unless they can produce very concrete evidence in their favour. A genuinely critical approach to the text will begin by being critical of its own assumptions and theories. Historical scepticism has no prior claim to be considered. Doubt is no less prone to bias and naivety than confidence. Many of the elaborate theories spun in previous generations about Luke's motive for writing, though considered highly plausible at the time, are now, in the light of a more sober assessment, reckoned to be speculative fantasies.

In the second place, it is absolutely clear that Luke wrote Acts with a purpose and selected his material in order to fulfil his aim. There is nothing dishonourable about that. Indeed, he himself comes clean, and invites his readers to consider these things for themselves (Lk. 1:1–4). If necessary, they should check the accuracy of what they are reading. It is a peculiarly modern fallacy to assume that because a message is presented in such a way that it leads to commitment it is necessarily incompatible with historical accuracy.

There is no logic in such reasoning. Given both Luke's stated purpose and the nature of the message, one might presume that he would double his efforts not to distort the story at any point.

However, it is equally clear that he was not attempting merely to present a series of chronological happenings in the life of the early Church. He selected some and left others out. He wanted to convince his readers of the truth of the message, not simply give them an interesting account of unrelated events. Hence the Book of Acts possesses a structure and highlights particular themes.

One of those themes is the encounter between faith in a crucified and risen Messiah and other faiths. What actually happened when the first Christians told other people what they believed was God's final truth? Acts gives an account of this encounter. We may take it that the stories told there are representative of many others which made up the life and witness of the first Christian community.

I would like to focus on two of these crucial encounters: with Jewish people and with the followers of contemporary philosophies and cults. In many ways they are representative of people of different religious, political and philosophical convictions whom Christians have had the privilege of witnessing to down the ages. How they went about it in the period of the apostles is highly significant for our own practice today.

Somewhat arbitrarily, but in order to have a manageable block of material to look at, I intend to consider only the last twelve chapters of Acts. These describe the journeys of Paul and his companions from Thessalonica to Athens, Corinth and Ephesus on his second missionary journey; his third missionary journey to Asia Minor and Greece; and the events surrounding his arrest in Jerusalem and his final journey to Rome.

Encounter with the Jews

Because of the tragic way in which relationships between Christians and Jews have developed down the centuries, due as much as anything to sadly misguided interpretations of the New Testament by some Christians, it is hard to understand today how close the two communities would have been in the middle part of the first century.

Christians still went to the synagogues to worship the one, living God (Acts 26:11). It was the apostle Paul's invariable policy to go to the synagogue as soon as possible after entering a city (Acts 17:2). He in particular continued, in a number of ways, to identify himself as a member of the Jewish faith. He claimed still to be a Pharisee (Acts 23:6). He was willing, in order to dispel misunderstandings and demonstrate a certain loyalty to the law, to go through the ceremony of ritual purification (Acts 21:20–6). He commended Ananias as 'a devout observer of the law and highly respected by all the Jews' who were living in Damascus (Acts 22:12). During his defence before Felix, he identified himself as a member of the Jewish people, by fulfilling the regulations of the law to give alms, to present offerings in the temple and to maintain himself ritually pure (Acts 24:17–18). Finally, before Festus and Agrippa he reiterated that he belonged to the Jewish race and that faith in Jesus was in no way incompatible with being a Jew (Acts 26:5ff.).

We find echoed in Acts the incontrovertible fact that there were many different groups within Judaism at the time, each one with its own distinctive interpretations of the traditions. One of the most notable points of disagreement occurred between the Pharisees and the Sadducees over the resurrection (Acts 23:6–8). Also, the Pharisees believed in the possibility of new revelations from God (Acts 23:9). They were, therefore, theoretically more open to the reality of Jesus Christ than the powerful and conservative Sadducees.

Paul's main defence before the Roman authorities was that the dispute between him and some of the leaders in Jerusalem had to do with the way the Scriptures should be interpreted (Acts 24:14). This was hardly a matter for the governing bodies, seeing that disagreements over interpretation were already current in Judaism. In other words, Paul argued that he was part of a situation where debate, controversy and different parties were contained within one people. There was no one fixed way of being a Jew and fulfilling the ancient obligations to God.

It follows from this that Paul, quite naturally, presented faith in Christ as a perfectly legitimate way of interpreting the meaning of Jewish faith: 'I worship the God of our fathers as a follower of the Way, which they call a sect. I believe everything that agrees with the Law and that is written in the Prophets, and I have the same hope in God as these men' (Acts 24:14–15). He affirmed that he continued to be meticulous about observing the law: 'I strive always to keep my conscience clear before God and man' (Acts 24:16). Hence, he saw no contradiction between honouring the law of God and his faith in Jesus, who came to fulfil, not abrogate, that law. Clearly, in the eyes of Paul the Way was a perfectly legitimate interpretation and development of his people's faith. He defended his views by rejecting the accusation that his teaching was an unacceptable innovation or new fashion. On the contrary, it was a sound interpretation of God's revelation in the light of further revelation.

It seems to me that, in thinking about relationships between Jewish people and Christians, this position is supremely important. Of course, it is not easy to maintain today, because of the swift and dramatic separation of the Jewish and Christian communities during the latter half of the first century. Mutual antagonism makes it hard to see that both belong to the same stock (as indeed Paul eloquently argued in his famous metaphor of the olive tree – Rom. 11:17–24).

Moreover, following the uprisings of AD 66–70 and 135, Judaism itself became much less fluid. It inclined more to consolidate that one interpretation of its essence which at that time was still left to it, namely a religion of obedience to the Torah, as that had been handed down since the days of the Great Synagogue in the times of Ezra and Nehemiah. Persecution at the hands of the Romans made the Jewish nation less likely to fulfil its mandate to take the knowledge of God to the nations. While the Christians, finding some opposition to the message of the gospel among Jews, had increasingly turned to the Gentiles with the good news of Jesus.

However, the point at issue here is whether at that crucial time when the two communities were going their separate ways, only one of them had (and still has) the right to decide what it means to be a true Jew. The burden of much of the New Testament, not least the apostolic preaching as recorded in Acts, is that the belief that Jesus is the Messiah, predestined to die in order that sins might be forgiven and raised to new life so that the hope of *shalom* might be fulfilled, is an entirely legitimate way of interpreting the whole of Jewish history.

The situation between the two communities, of course, is much more complex than that. If the early communities of the Way had merely been what the lawyer Tertullus described them as, namely 'the Nazarene sect' (Acts 24:5; also Acts 28:22), there might not have been such a heated controversy between them. They might have simply taken their place among the many other Jewish sects of the time. However, because of the way they saw Jesus in relation to the God whom they knew and served, they were committed to interpreting the Way as the only legitimate interpretation of the Jewish faith.

This is made clear in the last major speech recorded in Acts, the one which seems to be directed almost exclusively to King Agrippa (Acts 26:2), although there were many others present, high-ranking members of both the Jewish community and the Roman garrison in Caesarea. Indeed, the setting, away from Jerusalem in the headquarters of the Roman occupation of Palestine, is itself significant for what Paul had to say. No doubt he spoke in Greek (contrast the use of Aramaic in Jerusalem – Acts 21:40) to a person who had strong connections with the ruling Romans, being the brother-in-law of the former procurator, Felix. Though Agrippa was a Jew, and had been given the right to appoint the high priest, he had deeply offended them by building a palace overlooking the temple in Jerusalem. Later he sided with the Romans in the great uprising which led to the sack of Jerusalem by Titus in AD 70. In the context, then, Paul's emphasis on being sent to the Gentiles (Acts 26:17) is entirely appropriate for the situation in which he found himself.

The point of real controversy between the two communities was the assumption made by the Christians that the message of the gospel was equally for the highly religious Jews and for the superstitious Gentiles (Acts 26:17–20). Both, though clearly in different ways and for different reasons, needed to come to the living God, amending their ways in conformity with God's true will. Not unnaturally the Jews, who sought to be strictly faithful to God's commandments as they understood them, resented being told that 'serving God day and night' (Acts 26:7; cf. Lk. 2:37) in the rituals prescribed by the holy law of God was not enough. They needed to recognise that in the resurrection of Jesus from the dead a new creation was dawning.

The God of their fathers was continuing to perform mighty acts. A wonderful event, fulfilling the same Scriptures which they all believed, had taken place in the recent past in their midst. God wanted his people to acknowledge and enjoy the benefits of his further offer of salvation. Paul himself, as the strictest of Jews, was a living testimony to this (Acts 22:14).

Some Christians today suggest that there are two parallel ways of relating to God, who maintains two covenants, one with the Jewish people and another with the Gentiles. Such a notion, attractive as it may be in fostering harmony between Christians and Jews, two groups that have become polarised and estranged from one another, has no support in the New Testament. It could not, for it would mean dividing the one people of God.

Much mischief has been done by referring to the Church as 'the new Israel'. This is a misunderstanding of how the early Christians saw themselves in relationship to the God who had revealed himself through his people Israel. The immediate purpose of sharing the gospel with the Jews was so that they might become the true community of the Messiah. Paul's purpose in going to the synagogue was to persuade his fellow Jews that their Scriptures had been fulfilled. He argued first that the Messiah promised in the Law and the Prophets had to suffer and rise from the dead; and, secondly, that as Jesus had done both these things, he must be the Messiah (Acts 17:2–3).

Judaism is essentially a messianic faith, i.e. one which trusts God to fulfil his promises to create a new heaven and a new earth marked by his reign of righteousness and peace. It is a longing that God's kingdom would come for the whole of humanity, as a healing of the nations. Israel was intended to be a witness to and the first-fruits of that new creation, whose birth was dependent upon the willingly assumed suffering of God's righteous servant (Isa. 42:1–4), the utterly unique 'child of the four names' (Isa. 9:6), who would then be vindicated by passing from death to new life.

The Church was quite simply Israel, i.e. that same community called to bear witness to God's promises and God's acts for the sake of the whole of his creation. The 'holy child' (or servant, the same word translates both in Greek, cf. Acts 3:13; 4:27–30) had come, suffered and been vindicated in the resurrection, an event no one could deny. This was the nub of the question: the resurrection was a fact to be witnessed to, not just a hope to be awaited. Even the pagan Roman governor, Festus, saw this as the substance of the Christian message: 'a dead man named Jesus whom Paul claimed was alive' (Acts 25:19).

The dispute between the two communities, then, centres on the heart of their witness to God. Without a recognition that the kingdom is already operating (although in a hidden form and in weakness) through the one offering of the Son to the Father, who gladly accepts him, witness to God is converted into a religion at whose heart is ethnic identity, fulfilment of the law to please God, and worship at the holy places. It was these three elements that Paul was accused of denying and desecrating: 'This is the man who teaches all men everywhere against our people and our law and this place' (Acts 21:28).

There is a sense in which the accusation is at least partly true, for the gospel has completely transposed the importance of ethnicity, it has radically revised the place of the law and has eliminated the need for holy places. In the sphere of the resurrection the Christian's basic identity is as a member of a multi-national community, made a holy people by faith in the one saviour given for all people; the law is obeyed from the inside of a person's being, rather than as an external code; and places have no particular sanctity about them, and therefore cannot be defiled.

The reaction of Jewish people throughout the Roman Empire to the message of the gospel was very mixed. It went all the way from the Jewish community in Berea who 'received the message with great eagerness', many believing (Acts 17:10–12), to the Jews from the province of Asia who stirred up a riot in Jerusalem against Paul and the four men who had taken the Nazirite vow (Acts 21:27ff.; cf. Acts 18:18). On the one hand, dialogue with Paul and checking the Scriptures led first to a re-evaluation of accepted interpretations and then to faith in Christ. On the other hand, the mere presence of Paul in Jerusalem led to a fanatical desperation to see him killed (Acts 23:12ff.). Perhaps this was one of the first of many examples, which can be paralleled in all religions (certainly including Christianity), of the ferocity which 'the guardians of the truth' can unleash against those seen as deviants. Though the very first was, of course, Paul himself (Acts 26:10–11).

There can be little doubt, whatever may be the verdict of people today, that the early Christians were not inhibited from proclaiming a message that might cause dissension among communities and might lead to their own imprisonment and suffering. They did not temporise, nor cease to preach, even when forbidden to do so. In Paul's words, their overriding concern was to accomplish the ministry received from the Lord Jesus, 'to testify to the gospel of the grace of God' (Acts 20:24, RSV).

Encounter with philosophies and cults

PAUL IN ATHENS

In his account of Paul's time in Athens (Acts 17:16ff.), Luke goes to the main point straightaway. Of all the things that provoked and concerned Paul more than any others were the idols and images he saw all around him. He was concerned primarily not with slavery, nor poverty, nor the beauty of the architecture, nor the splendour of the learning in Athens, but with the false religiosity.

As well as his customary entry into the local synagogue (as in Thessalonica and Berea), about which this time Luke tells us nothing more, Paul also went into the market-place to converse with 'those who happened to be there' (perhaps the stall-holders, shoppers, or people simply meeting to talk to one another or 'watch the world go by').

Luke does not say that Paul entered into a dialogue with these people, in which both parties would mutually enrich the faith of the other. Rather, he states that Paul argued with them, presumably about what is true and what is false. It was a kind of disputation, in which Paul started from the assumption that the religion of the Athenians was partially based on ignorance, partially wrong.

The burden of his message among those who, presumably, were not 'God-fearing' Gentiles was Jesus and the resurrection (while his message to the synagogue congregations had centred on Jesus, the Messiah).

We may deduce that the theme of *Jesus and the resurrection* was aimed at convincing the Athenians of the following important affirmations:

a) Historical events are crucial to a right understanding of God.
b) The only image of God which is allowed is that of Jesus Christ of Nazareth, who perfectly represents Him (Col. 1:15; Heb. 1:3).
c) Death is not *survived* by a mysterious human essence called the soul. Rather it is *conquered*, so that a complete physical transformation may take place. In this way Paul raised physical existence to a position of crucial importance, over against the Greek denial. By implication he rejected any use made of religion to favour the spiritual over the material or the sacred over the secular.

The 'philosophers', in response, tried to fit Paul's message into the parameters of their own basic assumptions. Firstly, *good philosophy requires good oratory*: Paul was only a babbler. It may well be that he was hesitant in his delivery, or not entirely at home with the sophisticated language of the Athenian élite. Secondly, *good philosophy supersedes bare theology*: Paul's message had no intellectual credibility. What was foreign was inferior, mere superstition. Thirdly, *good philosophy is always looking for new ideas*: its origin is the creative imagination of human thought.

It was precisely because of this third premise that the 'philosophers' were willing to hear more from Paul. Perhaps he would bring some new concept or fresh, exciting idea that they could weave into the multi-coloured fabric of their own understanding of life.

There were two aspects of Paul's message which were new and, for that reason, excited curiosity. Firstly, *Jesus*: his name was unfamiliar (being Hebrew and not Greek). Moreover, he was (or had been) a concrete person of the recent past, not a mythological figure of remote, primordial times. Finally, it was claimed that his death on a Roman cross (Romans were despised by the Greeks) was the means of salvation for every living person. Secondly, the *resurrec-*

tion: an entirely new concept, which they wanted to test to see whether it fitted into their scheme of things, or not.

They confessed that these were 'strange things', of which they had no previous experience. Indeed, no natural revelation or inference about a transcendent reality would ever have begun to give them an inkling of these truths. They were perplexed. They could not grasp the meaning, even less the significance of the message. Paul returned to the preaching of Jesus and the resurrection at the end of his Areopagus address: 'the man he has appointed . . . raising him from the dead' (v.31).

It was the message of the resurrection, rather than the 'creation theology' of the main part of Paul's address, which many of his hearers rejected. So, Paul did not compromise or temporise his message to fit the world-view of the Athenian 'opinion-formers'. He preached a scandalous and costly message, which called the Athenians to renounce their mistaken religious views, in order to be able to enjoy fellowship with the true God (cf. 1 Thess. 1:9).

Paul begins with an observation – 'in every way you are very religious' – which he had gained from looking at what the Athenians had made most prominent. Even though many of them may have been sceptical about these things (that would accord with part of their intellectual tradition), they took precautions not to offend the gods.

Paul's observation is based on the following facts:

a) There were many different objects of worship all along the sides of the roads.
b) There was one altar dedicated to 'an unknown god'. The purpose of this one altar may have been to cover any god not specifically recognised by name in any other shrine, or it may have been that the Athenians had an inkling of one supreme being (one inexpressible Other behind all the gods).

Both these possible interpretations of the unknown god are borne out by what Paul says next: 'what you worship as something unknown . . . ' Firstly, they worship this god, both because of a desire to fulfil their religious duties by honouring all beings who may control their destiny, and in case, through neglect, they incur their displeasure and harm. Their religiosity (or superstition – where is the boundary?) is marked by their need to cover every eventuality. Secondly, what they worship is, however, unknown, for one cannot know of the existence of a being without knowing what he/she is like. So the unknown remains a something, until disclosed. Self-disclosure presupposes a personal being who either acts or speaks (or both) in a way which is recognisable.

It is obvious, then, given the interest of the Athenians in religious matters, that Paul would go on immediately to declare what, in spite of the highest wisdom and philosophical sophistication of almost any age, the people did not know, having demonstrated their ignorance already in the matter of Jesus and the resurrection.

The most high God (the highest being or God behind the gods) is distinguished by three great facts:

a) He is the creator of everything that exists. Therefore, there is no god beyond the creator. (This was actually denied by many who subscribed to some form of Gnostic belief, on the grounds that, by the act of creating what is corruptible in itself, a god would demonstrate his inferiority.)
b) He is Lord of heaven and earth. Therefore, he alone controls all that is – nature, history and destiny.
c) He does not live in shrines made by humans. Therefore, he cannot be limited to anything that humans can control. God is confined neither to certain spaces in the world nor to certain times. Therefore, there is nothing specially holy (sacral) about any place, activity, person or event. The fact of creation demythologises the holy, making all things holy (and consequently all things secular – under the heaven, on the earth).

Paul continues with a number of further statements about

the one, true God. Firstly, 'he is not served by human hands, as if he needed anything'. Human beings cannot do favours to, nor win favours from God by their actions, whether these are the offering of sacrifices (as in primal religions) or the fulfilling of good works (as in common folk religion). The relationship between God and humanity is non-instrumental: God cannot be persuaded to serve our needs either through prayer or through selfless service to others or through the holiness of our lives. Any idea of putting God in our debt (in a subtle way, the basis of prosperity teaching) is a mark of pagan religion.

Secondly, 'he himself gives all men life and breath and everything else'. We depend wholly on God, not the other way round. Therefore, the mark of a true relationship to God is thanksgiving and praise for his 'mighty acts'.

Thirdly,

> From one man he made every nation of men, that they should inhabit the whole earth; and he determined the times set for them and the exact places where they should live. God did this so that men would seek him and perhaps reach out for him and find him, though he is not far from each one of us. 'For in him we live and move and have our being.' As some of your own poets have said, 'We are his offspring.'

This long statement can be broken down into several short, sharp affirmations:

a) 'From one man he made every nation.' Humanity comes from a common stock. There is more that unites us than divides us. Hence, the validity of different cultures cannot be a reason for the legitimacy of different religions. We are all made for the same one, true God.
b) 'He determined the exact places where they should live.' This does not mean any more than that each ethnic group needs the space to develop its own traditions and culture, without interference from others.

It is the divine imperative against unlawful encroachment, and remains true even in multi-cultural societies. In other words, the determining is spatial not temporal – not for all time.

c) 'So that [people] would seek [God] . . . and find him.' This is the purpose for which all peoples have been created. The emphasis in Paul's statement, unlike that common in contemporary inter-faith theology, is not on the seeking, but on the finding. It is the end of the journey, not the journey itself, which is important. Seeking may be in the right direction, in which case it will bear fruit; or it may be wholly in the wrong direction, in which case it will not end up in truth and life. The seeking in itself guarantees nothing. Undoubtedly, some do find the God of whom Paul speaks, usually when, dissatisfied with the religion of their culture, they probe beyond it.

d) 'He is not far from each one of us.' God's closeness is predicated on two great truths. Firstly, we exist because he exists ('in him we live and move and have our being'). Our life, breath and actions all depend on his sustaining power. God is no absent prime-mover. His Spirit is everywhere activating life and making it possible on a moment-to-moment basis. Thus *is* the God of creation. Secondly, we are like God, created in his image ('We are his offspring'). There is, therefore, no infinite divide between the transcendent and everyday reality. This fact is, of course, crucial if there is to be any personal relationship between God and human beings.

Paul finishes speaking about the God whom he declares to the Athenians by drawing a number of negative conclusions: God cannot be represented by images created by human hands, nor does he infuse them with some spark of the divine, nor does he allow that our 'understandable' ignorances are minor matters of unimportance (in Romans 1 he uses stronger language).

God is utterly patient with our desire to create our gods in our own image; but not for ever. The proper response of the 'very religious' is not to seek further understanding or enlightenment, but to repent. The call to repentance implies moral culpability and failure. The creation of images is not a neutral pastime. It is the result of human arrogance and pride. These will be judged.

Up to this point (as in Rom. 1:18ff.), Paul is moving in the orbit of Hebrew faith. Now he concludes with three statements which lie at the heart of the Christian gospel: the incarnation ('the man'), the Messiahship of Jesus (whom 'he has appointed'), and the resurrection ('by raising him from the dead'). The false religiosity of the human race, displayed in the idolatry of human-created images, will be judged by the one and only true visible image (*eikon*) of the invisible God (Col. 1:15; 2 Cor. 4:4; 1 Tim. 1:17).

The resurrection became for the Athenians both a point of fascination and a point of disruption. It promises new life and hope, but also implies the utter particularity of the Christian gospel: God has only ever raised one person from corruption to incorruption on this earth. The uniqueness of the message is that the transformation of all things, signalled for the end of time, has in principle already happened.

The response was that some mocked and some believed; a typical consequence of what happened wherever the gospel was declared. Perhaps to convey the equality of the sexes before God and their equal ability to have faith, Luke mentions by name one man and one woman who believed.

So ends Paul's epic visit to the great city of Athens and his confrontation with its philosophy and religiosity. These remain two of the greatest barriers to belief, represented today perhaps by Enlightenment culture (philosophy) and common religion (religiosity).

PAUL IN EPHESUS

The religion of Artemis was a classic example in the ancient world of the way in which common religious needs are fulfilled at a popular level. The shrines which were made by the silversmiths (they were also made in terracotta and marble) had a representation of the goddess in a small niche. This effigy was believed to possess the life of the goddess, so that anyone who kept it in their home, to reverence it, or wore it around their neck or on their wrist in the form of an amulet, for continuous protection, would be able to receive for themselves a portion of the divine life.

Although Artemis is the name of the Greek goddess who was a daughter of Zeus and Leto and twin sister of Apollo, and who was the patron of the moon and hunting, in Ephesus the name was assimilated to an ancient fertility goddess, represented by a woman with many breasts. Devotion to the goddess was widespread, and the religion which surrounded her was the established belief of most of the Ephesian population.

Much of the city's prosperity was built on trade carried out with the numerous pilgrims who descended on the place from far and wide, particularly during the special festival of the Spring Equinox. The shrines, in particular, would have been taken home as living symbols of the divine power which guarantees a harmonious and successful life.

The temple to Artemis was considered to be one of the seven wonders of the ancient world. It was a great building, measuring over 400 feet long by nearly 250 feet wide. It was supported by 100 columns, rising to 56 feet. It was richly endowed through the offerings which the pilgrims and worshippers bestowed. This wealth supported a vast number of temple officials. It may be, therefore, that one of the reasons why Artemis was considered to be great (Acts 19:28,34) was that she was, in a manner of speaking, a great employer of human labour.

It is not surprising that Demetrius, one of the creators of silver shrines, should see the danger to the entire religious and economic structure of the city of the message that Paul and the other followers of the Way were proclaiming. It was not difficult for him to arouse others in allied trades to confront this threat head on.

When Paul returned to Ephesus after an initial, brief, first visit (Acts 18:19), he found there already a small group of disciples (Acts 19:1). They had been formed presumably as a result of the preaching of Apollos, Priscilla and Aquila (Acts 18:24ff.). He continued the ministry of Apollos, who had gone to Corinth, first in the synagogue for three months and then for two years in the lecture hall of Tyrannus. During this time he would have been able to inform large numbers of people, including no doubt many of the pilgrims (cf. Acts 19:10), of the content of the message about Jesus and the kingdom of God. His method, not unlike that of the philosophers, was by open public lectures followed by discussion and debate (Acts 19:9).

His influence on the city, however, did not end there. He also carried out what today we would call a healing ministry, including the exorcism of malign and destructive spirits. Moreover, the power of the faith that he represented was visibly manifest in two further occurrences. Firstly, seven Jewish exorcists found themselves unable to use the name of Jesus in order to carry out their rites. Their spurious incantations, 'In the name of Jesus, whom Paul preaches' (Acts 19:14), were shown up. Secondly, a number of people who practised magic arts publicly burned the main source of their practices, the scrolls which were inscribed with special magical charms.

The disciples did not attack either the magic or the religion of Artemis directly (cf. Acts 19:37). Rather, it was those who practised these things who clearly saw that the two ways of relating to unseen spiritual forces were quite incompatible. Nevertheless, their challenge to the popular religiosity of the people and the financial gain which resulted from it was unmistakable.

Whether or not Demetrius was genuinely concerned about the religion of Artemis or about the honour and fame of the city associated with her name or about what would happen to the culture and self-identity of the people if they no longer believed in her power, or whether he was only interested in the potential economic disaster which he and other traders might face if the customary religion of the people collapsed is not the point. He saw clearly, as did the practitioners of magic, that a choice had to be made between Jesus and the new order of things which he represented and the common religious beliefs that the ordinary people had hitherto practised. Unlike some modern global religious ecumenists, they did not envisage any way of bringing the faith of Jesus and the faith of Artemis into some kind of creative harmony.

Some responded to the gospel by destroying their valuable assets, which were their means of livelihood, in spite of the insecurity for the future which such an action would have represented. Others responded by stirring up a riot, presumably with the intention of intimidating the followers of the Way, with the hope that they would leave the city as it had always been.

The purpose of this chapter is to show, from one historical account of the way the early Christian communities lived their faith, that they were convinced that they had an overriding mandate to persuade all who would listen that Jesus Christ alone was both the true judge between right and wrong and also the one authenticated by God to save people from false beliefs and destructive practices. Whatever else may be said about their zeal to spread the word of God as they understood it, it was not based on a desire to gain thereby worldly power in any of its forms. The Christian faith, once the issues about Gentiles observing elements of the Jewish law had been settled, was not in any way tied to the self-interests of a particular ethnic group or nation.

In spite of its long association with colonial expansion from the West, the Church today may, and indeed must, return to the purer, less self-regarding motives of the earliest Christian groups in its calling to tell out the good news of Jesus and the kingdom of God. Perhaps it needs especially to recapture the meaning of *dialogue* as used by Luke in the Acts of the Apostles, namely the method of discussing the merits of a particular set of convictions with a view to persuading others to commit themselves in a similar way. Unless it shares the apostles' underlying assumptions about evangelism, it is difficult to see how the Church of today can be considered authentically 'apostolic'.

9

Freedom from Religion for Freedom

'He has sent me to proclaim freedom for the prisoners and recovery of sight for the blind, to release the oppressed.'
—**Jesus of Nazareth**

'My chains fell off, my heart was free, I rose, went forth and followed thee.'
—**Charles Wesley**

'They have nothing to lose but their chains.'
—**Karl Marx**

The time has come to try to draw together the many strands of the argument so far and attempt some firm conclusions. I began with the observation that, if religion is understood in a wide sense, many people, even in a secularised society, maintain religious beliefs with some persistence: many more, certainly, than those who belong openly to one or another religious community. The number of religious believers is in direct proportion to the elasticity of the definition of religion. People who are convinced that any religion is better than none, simply because the one-dimensional existence presupposed by consistent secularism demeans and trivialises human life, are tempted to include in their understanding of religion all kinds of serious commitment beyond the self.

The problem with the wide definition of religion is that it tends to patronise those people who have either consciously opted for a humanist view of life, or who have simply drifted away from religious beliefs (both the atheist and the agnostic), by telling them that, whatever their conviction, it has a religious dimension. However, we truly respect people when we allow them the integrity of actually believing what they profess to believe.

There are indeed a great number of people living in contemporary post-industrial societies who do not believe there is any reality beyond the visible world that in any way affects what they do or think in this life. There are others who live *as if* there was nothing tangible the other side of human communities and the physical world. Both groups live on the assumption that all that is is confined within the closed four walls of the material universe. I believe that no one else has the right to suggest that that is not what they really believe, even if living consistently on the basis of such a conviction may prove exceedingly difficult.

Nevertheless, the majority probably still do subscribe to some kind of religious belief or other. We have seen that a residual belief in God and prayer, as well as the occasional attendance at a religious ceremony, often has magical overtones. By this we mean a relationship with the divine which seems to be both fitful and mechanical. God is around and able to help, when the normal mechanisms of life break down. He is benevolently disposed towards us, as long as we have done our best to be kind to others, or at least refrained from harming them.

The magical view of religion (see chapter 1) is essentially functional, that is it views contact with a sacred world to be useful in circumstances like bereavement, serious sickness, unmerited suffering, local or national tragedies (such as train crashes, boats sinking, football supporters being crushed to death, or war). Religion also serves to give meaning to the joyous moments of life: the celebration of new life, marriage, financial success, recovery from an operation. In both cases, sorrow and gladness, religion performs the role of helping us deal with the uncertainty of life. It is a shield that is available to protect us from harm, whenever the various circumstances of life have moved beyond our power to control.

The impact of a secular view of life

Perhaps the majority of people who live in what have been called 'post-modern' societies hover uncertainly between a religious and an irreligious view of existence, between the sacred and the secular. Understandably, they want to hedge their bets: not to be thought stupid or weak by believing in a spiritual realm, but not to be arrogant enough to declare that the sacred is nothing but an invention for people who lack the courage to believe that there is nothing in life or death beyond the human. Most of us live as if the universe were a desert island, surrounded by an infinite, uninhabited sea, on which we have to manage by ourselves as best we may. But, at the same time, we launch bottles into the ocean and send out smoke signals in the hope that there may be a passing ship that will rescue us from our solitude.

A secularised view of the world has given rise to two powerful traditions. The first is *the irreligious critique of religion*. We have never seen a ship. We create the illusion of ships because we have not yet learned how to cope on our own. Once we have fully explored the island, and we have a comprehensive explanation for everything we find there, we will be delivered from the irrational fears of the unknown which make rescue by a ship such an attractive possibility.

The theory of the origin of religion which sees it as a projection of our needs, whether these are some kind of compensation for misfortune in this life, or justification for the privileges we enjoy, or for strength in times of stress and helplessness, or for the assuaging of guilt-feelings, has much truth in it. Nobody who wants to defend the place of religion in life can afford to ignore this kind of explanation. It has the undoubted merit of demonstrating the impossibility of facing both ways at once: of believing, most of the time, that the natural order is closed to all outside intervention, making the idea of a God an impossible hypothesis, yet at the same time affirming a sacred order which provides a depth to life lacking in a purely materialist view. It is fascinating how many Christians who claim to reinterpret the faith 'radically' seek to escape a consistently naturalistic view of the world by the use of language which evokes the memory of a reality beyond the material, even though, on their assumptions, there cannot be anything or anyone there: words like transcendence, myth, symbol, relational, the sacred dimension, ultimate reality.

They are basically secularists, but wholly inconsistent ones. They are in fact using language in a magical way, hoping that the incantation of words, which once possessed a deep meaning within a particular culture, will somehow carry over some of that meaning, even when the original reality to which the words pointed is no longer believed to exist literally.

Robin Gill gives a good example of this kind of magical trick when he says, 'an expression of faith will be seen as a vital, but transient and culture bound, attempt to articulate what finally goes beyond articulation'; 'it is only our relationship to God, not the verbal expression of this relationship, that is constant' (Gill 1989:12, 50). He makes it plain that he does not believe that there can be any literal correspondence between the way we describe an unseen reality and the reality itself: 'like all relationships a relationship to God cannot adequately and without considerable distortion be reduced to words' (Gill 1989:146). But the conclusion he draws cannot be borne out by the assumption he makes, for there would be no way of knowing that distortion had taken place. The phrase, 'relationship to God', is left hanging in the air, unconnected to any identifiable object.

The full-blooded secularist is more honest. He or she is also more courageous in denying to religion a role in meeting those apparent needs which a one-dimensional view of life ignores. There is something hollow about a view of religion which sees it merely in a functional way, however worthy may be the cause for which it is pressed into service: for example, giving the basis for an ethical consensus in society, or bringing together human communities, or providing a cushion against stress, or preventing irrational outbreaks of violence, or providing motivation for the uncalculating service of others. In these kinds of way religion is reduced to a commodity, at our service, to use in any way which we see fit. Either belief in God in a particular way is true, in the sense that such a God exists and corresponds to the way we see him, or the consistent secularist is right to dismiss all religious talk as the invention of those who have not yet dared to take the step of abandoning their illusions. Attempted half-way houses are built on shifting sands. They are bound to fall apart.

Let no modern defender of world religions ignore the powerful critique of religious life and language unleashed by the secular mind, taking refuge in talk of mystical, indefinable experiences. Today, emphatically, we live in a post-secular age. We may not try to counter the consequences of secularism by seeking to bring together the religions, as if they were allies against a common enemy. In their dismissal of much religious talk as double-think, secularists may paradoxically be much closer to the real God than many a religious devotee. They, at least, insist that we keep the question of truth firmly on the agenda. If it were not for the fact that Christians have so often reduced their faith to mere religion, they might find the real secularist much closer to the kingdom of God than they can imagine.

Having spoken partly in favour of the secularist outlook, we must also insist that those who hold to it are less than honest when they remain optimistic in the face of inescapably nihilistic pressures. Classical Marxism, for example, has only survived as a utopian alternative to the ruthlessness of a free-market economy, whose only rules are competition, profit and the survival of the fittest, by changing the direction of 'illusory' hope from the beyond of space to the beyond of time, from the invisible world to the future world.

The possibility that there might be what the Marxists call a 'classless society' in which the freedom of all is guaranteed by the freedom of each, and in which each will contribute fully and freely to the needs of the common good, should also be criticised in the same terms as have been applied to religion. It is an *illusion*, based only on the strong desire that it may happen. It is *opium*, which partially alleviates present suffering. It is *compensation* for the harsh struggle that must take place before the utopian world can be brought into being. In the light of history, it is a false *inversion* of reality: for to believe that the capitalist mode of production is doomed to internal disintegration by the logic of its own success, or that a communist society is destined in the nature of events to replace it, is to place a superstitious faith in the progressive nature of historical forces. In the last resort it gives more credence to the Hegelian *idea* of the inevitable negation of what has already negated the past than to the real, *material* world. On what grounds, other than a 'transcendent' faith, should one accept that a communist, rather than a capitalist, ordering of society is the final climax of human history?

The second powerful tradition is *the widespread relativistic approach to truth*. We have examined the causes and consequences of what has become perhaps the most widely accepted axiom of the modern world, in so far as it is modern, that nothing beyond the world of scientific experimentation and confirmation can be known truly. This assumption has been accepted as absolutely valid by many people from a Christian background who propose a greater degree of coming together of the world religions. For our purpose it is important to look closely at the way in which this relativistic assumption about all facets of life except the strictly scientific has led these people to proclaim the absolute necessity of a pluralist view of religions.

We are dealing here with pluralism as a theory of knowing, not with a plurality of beliefs as a reality of modern societies. This distinction is crucial, for, although I argue that the former is impossible, the latter is a necessary outcome of the Christian faith itself. Though the history of the gradual toleration of religious differences and the codifying of laws which guarantee rights of religious freedom is somewhat complex, it has much to do with the Nonconformist conscience and the willingness of Christian minorities and Jews to suffer abuse, imprisonment and death for the freedom to express their beliefs.

The stand against religious conformity and discrimination antedated the Enlightenment's powerful attack on all forms of religion by more than two hundred years (in the case of the Jews by very much longer), and must therefore be counted primarily as the fruit of faith, rather than doubt. One of the positive results of confining religious belief to the sphere of private conviction has, perhaps, been the freedom engendered for people to change their religious allegiance, if they so desire. Such freedom is still only fully recognised in those nations which have passed through a deeply secularising experience. In this sense the secular is both the consequence of (in part) and an ally for the Christian gospel. In the light of previous religious wars and the continuing religious intolerance of some nations against minority beliefs, the withdrawal of all legal sanctions against particular religious beliefs is a great blessing. Plurality in the practice of religious faith accords with the Christian view of God, for, if he were to coerce belief, he would deny his own creation and sabotage faith.

However, pluralism as a theory of religious belief is wholly different. It finds a basis in that tradition of philosophical thought which makes a fundamental distinction between the real and the appearance of the real. This, in turn, is derived from the deistic assumption that the ultimately real (the one true God) cannot be truly known through what has been revealed. It is claimed (as a matter of dogma) that final truth cannot be mediated through propositional statements, for these are inevitably human approximations to what we apprehend of the divine from our limited and distorted positions. Therefore, the real comes to us not directly, but in a codified form through mythological stories and symbols. Somehow we have to discern the footsteps of the divine in the tangled undergrowth of the images and language that human beings have created over the course of millennia.

Such an assumption, which is at the heart of the modern *Zeitgeist* (the spirit of the age), makes a plurality of beliefs not only inevitable, but for some a joyful discovery of the richness and diversity of paths to the ultimate reality. Now religions need not be in conflict any longer. For a partial apprehension to be converted into a wholeness of vision each needs the other. The acceptance of this assumption about truth has the happy outcome that religious human communities can unite around the common search for what is right, good and noble. Together we can tackle massive human problems, such as poverty, war and the environment, for we can be confident that our religious differences are ultimately a mirage, however real they may seem close at hand.

Although pluralism appears highly plausible to our culture, and academically respectable as a way of approaching the real, it is literally, and in other ways, an impossible belief. It is full of logical absurdities. It poses insurmountable theological problems. It leads to grave ethical dangers. We will look in turn at each of these vigorous challenges to the pluralist thesis.

The logical absurdity of pluralism

Firstly, because there is a built-in fallacy at the heart of pluralism, access to truth is simultaneously denied and affirmed. It is denied as a propositional revelation from a personal divine being. It is affirmed as the proposition that our apprehension of the divine is inevitably distorted. Why is this latter proposition not also distorted by a limited cultural viewpoint? Why is the affirmation of universal cultural relativity the only one guaranteed free of such relativity? There is no reason. The pluralist starts just as much with an autonomous and unverifiable belief as does the believer in propositional revelation. The main difference is that the former has not, as yet, been challenged by the culture to submit his or her belief to rigorous criticism.

Secondly, for pluralism to work the theory has to start from a non-cognitive experience, which is said in all cases to be the same in substance, though possibly different in outward expression. However, logically, the experience, which by definition goes beyond the appearance of the real, cannot be said to be the same as other experiences, for, if our apprehension of the object is always distorted, we cannot know what the object of experience really is. The most we can say, in a perfect expression of agnosticism, is that the experience is of that which is experienced.

Moreover, there is no way of knowing whether the ultimate reality is being experienced. All that we can say here is that experience is being interpreted in different ways, which in the case of the world's religions seem to be quite contradictory and incompatible. The point of reference – the religious experience – is quite arbitrary and cannot be defended against the relativist theory of historical and cultural contingency. When we start from an experience which cannot be conveyed truly in language, we end up inevitably with a tautology: all religion is a response to that which is responded to.

Thirdly, there is a confused epistemology. Pluralism is based on the false dichotomy between the ideal and the real, as it seeks to drive a wedge between the object of faith and the means which are used to describe it. The divorce between appearance and reality has overtones of Greek philosophical thought. We should not be surprised, then, that John Hick (one of the doyens of pluralism) declares that he follows the path of Greek rationality. Such a dichotomy, of course, makes knowledge impossible. Where there is no basis on which a true statement could be made, we are embarked upon an unending progression of doubt, which must lead to the precipice of complete nihilism.

There is, however, a true dichotomy which resolves the epistemological problem: the proper distinction between the partial and the whole – 'we know in part, then we shall know fully, even as we are fully known' (cf. 1 Cor. 13:12). It is only on the basis of being able to know truly, even if only partially, that it makes any sense to talk about distortion.

Fourthly, religious pluralism is maintained only at the cost of excluding certain beliefs. Naturally, in this way, it cannot be fully pluralist. It is a fact that pluralism can be declared an adequate interpretation of religious reality only if the central beliefs of certain religions are reinterpreted to mean something quite different from what the adherents of those religions have usually believed. In declaring, on the grounds of the present cultural consensus, what people ought and ought not to believe, the pluralist position has rightly been seen as imperialist and intolerant, the very characteristics which it denounces in the exclusivist claims of some religious traditions.

Therefore, in spite of appearances and claims to the contrary, pluralism is bound to be discriminatory and exclusivist. In the field of the theory of religions, then, it seems that we do not have a choice between an exclusivist and a pluralist position, between absolutism and tolerance, only between two different forms of exclusivism. This conclusion springs from the logic of all human thought, based as it must be in part on the necessity of antithesis.

Fifthly, in its desire to unite without excluding, and in its assumption that the same reality lies behind the variety of appearances of the real, pluralism is bound to deny what *is* the case (namely that at crucial points different religions espouse beliefs which contradict one another) in favour of what *must be* the case. This strand in the argument has led John Bowker to assert colourfully that 'the religions may, all of them, be entirely wrong in what they claim to be the ultimate case; but clearly, there's a lot more on the table here than a choice between margarine and butter' (1983:287).

The theological barriers to pluralism

Those who espouse a pluralist approach to religions usually maintain that, because today many of us live in close proximity to people of other faiths, our world is substantially different from the one our forebears knew. The reality of the 'global village', in which we are all conscious of the multiplicity of races, cultures and beliefs, makes it impossible to pretend any longer that any one religious tradition possesses an exclusive access to the final truth about the universe. Such people may still speak about the uniqueness of the Christian faith. However, this is not understood to mean 'the one and only' but 'the only one of its kind', implying that in this sense all religions are unique, just as all human beings are unique, because there is no one else the same.

In one sense it is true to say that we live in a wholly new situation with regard to the relationship between different faith communities. However, it is important to recognise where that newness lies. As far as the Christian community is concerned, it is not that religious diversity has been discovered for the first time, but the way in which that diversity is interpreted. As we have already seen, the early Church was acutely conscious that it was proclaiming that Jesus Christ is Lord in a world every bit as pluralist as our own. The apostle Paul refers directly to this fact in his first letter to the Christians in Corinth when he reminds them of their own first-hand experience that 'indeed there are many "gods" and many "lords"' (1 Cor. 8:5).

One of the major differences between the Christians of the first century and those contemporary Christians who maintain that our new situation forces us to re-evaluate our undertanding of other faiths, is that many of the former had actually experienced what it meant to live under the authority and power of 'other lords'. If the New Testament is to be believed, their conversion from a wide variety of religious beliefs and practices to the exclusive lordship of Jesus Christ was experienced as liberation from oppression. The vast majority of those who speak today in a positive way about religious pluralism have only experienced another faith from the outside.

It is perhaps ironic that these people seem, in their discussion of the issues, to approximate so closely to the beliefs of the Gnostic sects of the first and second centuries AD. Are they, I wonder, aware of the striking parallels? For example, they make the same implicit claim to have discovered an (esoteric) knowledge about ultimate reality. Arguments used against the 'myth' of Christian uniqueness depend upon them having access to a knowledge superior to that given to the apostles in their interpretation of the fact of Jesus Christ. That knowledge is said to come from a gradual expansion or evolution of consciousness about the world. The corollary is that now we have to leave behind the notion of exclusivity because it is based on a more primitive consciousness.

Then again, there is a striking similarity between the Gnostic and the modern view that the final truth about all things cannot possibly be revealed in particular, contingent circumstances. This, however, is precisely what the apostles claimed for the life, death and resurrection of the one man, Jesus of Nazareth.

Finally, the Gnostic conviction that there can be no direct contact between the noumenal world of the divine being and the phenomenal world of ordinary life is echoed in the emphasis laid upon religious experience as a means of being in touch with ultimate reality. The Gnostic belief was that the divine was so far removed from the transient, corruptible and ephemeral world of sense-perception that many mediators were needed to ascend from the one to the other. In contemporary pluralist thought the many experiences, each said to be equally valid, are somewhat equivalent to the many mediators of the divine reality. Moreover, in some traditions, both the mediators and the experiences are said to form different steps on a kind of ascending, cosmic ladder which brings the enlightened closer to the ultimate divine reality.

As a phenomenon, then, even though the language has changed considerably, the modern position on religious pluralism shares many assumptions with ancient Gnosticism. Both are far removed from the apostolic faith. Each assumption is bound to lead to the view that the central message of the New Testament, that 'in Christ all the fulness of the Deity lives in bodily form' (Col. 2:9), is, to put it mildly, a gross exaggeration.

The major difficulty for the pluralist, though rarely acknowledged openly and tackled, is that, in order to consign Christian claims to special revelation to the dustbin of history, one must possess a superior vantage-point (revelation) from which one is able to see that the former beliefs are no longer tenable. To discredit the historic Christian position, it is not sufficient merely to *assert* that modern consciousness has developed a new awareness of the unity of all religious faith. Such a procedure simply makes one judge and jury in favour of one's own case!

To put it another way, it is meaningless to say that the same divine or transcendent reality lies behind the different manifestations of religious devotion unless one has a clear concept of the nature of that reality. To pretend that the beyond can be experienced in terms of categories such as self-giving love, justice or the ultimately real is to fall back into a Greek mode of thinking which sets up the universal, abstract idea as the final truth. Surely this trend explains why Wilfred Cantwell Smith is also proud to declare himself 'an intellectual in the Greek tradition' (1987:182). Though one might wonder why he has apparently preferred Plato's world of universal ideas to Aristotle's insistence on antithesis.

God, however, cannot be defined by anything other than himself. To say that God is the equivalent of certain categories and then to discover that those categories describe the ultimate reality, which is God, is manifestly to argue in a circle. Of course it is true that we can only speak about God using concepts which are meaningful to us within our ordinary human experience. It is also true that these only approximate to the real nature of God and therefore need to be corrected. But this can only happen if God has manifested himself to us in a way which it is possible to recognise and talk about, that is to say in a human way. Indeed, we can only know that our language about God is faulty if we have a wholly reliable, linguistic disclosure of what God is really like.

The pluralist is caught in an unresolvable dilemma, which is particularly highlighted by John Hick's attempt to defend religious pluralism. His whole argument flows from the basic presupposition that 'the great world faiths embody different perceptions and conceptions of, and correspondingly different responses to, the Real or Ultimate from within the different cultural ways of being human' (Hick 1985:91). In line with this argument, 'Allah and Brahman are two ways in which limitless divine reality has been thought and experienced by different human mentalities formed by different intellectual frameworks and devotional techniques' (Hick 1985:96). How does he know this? Not on the basis of any divine disclosure of the actual contours of this limitless divine reality, for he is adamant 'that the language of revelation is out of place in discussions of religious pluralism'.

Hick is right in one sense, because to have any meaning a divine revelation must assume a correspondence between what is revealed and final truth, and thus may declare certain 'perceptions and conceptions' of the ultimate reality to be wrong. In another sense, however, religious pluralism requires some kind of disclosure to validate its basic premise. Thus Hick is totally disingenuous, when he says, 'we do not pretend to a cosmic vantage-point from which one could observe both Divine Reality in itself and different partial human awarenesses of it' (Hick 1985:97). In practice he assumes just such a vantage-point, for he *knows* that all perceptions of transcendence do in point of fact express the one divine reality. He claims exactly the same kind of knowledge as the orthodox believer, who says he knows that they do not all express the same divine reality.

Another grave problem for pluralists is that they have to

reinterpret all the different religions in ways that make them unrecognisable to the faith communities which practise them. To make discourse possible, a religion must be recognisable within certain boundaries, which are defined both by the living tradition of that religion, inherited from the past, and by the living community which is committed to that particular set of beliefs. There is no justification for an arbitrary, Humpty-Dumpty-like recasting of the faith, in order to make it less particular.

Of course, there is always a legitimate variety within each religion. But this can never be taken to the extreme of people both contradicting what has always been recognised as the fundamental heart of a faith and yet continuing to assert that they remain faithful adherents of it. Robin Gill is wrong in his strong emphasis on *divergent* beliefs and interpretations coming out of the New Testament. A *diversity* of ways of understanding the meaning of Christ, clearly evident in the pages of the New Testament, does not necessarily imply (as he seems to assume) the absence of a fundamental unity. The touchstone of the latter is that true pattern of faith which the apostles claim to have received from Christ and handed on to his disciples. They, at least, were perfectly clear that a distinction could be made between diversity and *deviation* (so, for example, Col. 2:6–23).

Gill admits that pluralism (implying a relative view of truth) has to be a necessary outcome of the premises from which he is working: 'doctrinal, ethical and structural pluralism of Christianity is a correlate of the elusive theistic relationship upon which it is based' (Gill 1989:148). This relationship, he asserts, is automatically distorted whenever it is articulated in human language. If this assumption were to be true, no one of course would be in any better position than anyone else to define the essential boundaries of the faith. He is wrong, however, to turn a philosophical proposition into a statement of contemporary historical fact, when he says that 'empirically there is no agreement amongst Churches which are or are not the essential boundaries' (148). Recent theological discussion among widely different

Churches, co-ordinated both by the World Council of Churches and world confessional bodies, on the sacraments, on ministry, on mission and evangelism, and on the apostolic faith itself, has shown a great measure of convergence, much more significant than the still outstanding divergences.

I suspect that Gill is confusing the opinions of individual theologians with the collective mind of the Church. This is borne out by his extraordinary claim that 'a sense of relativism is enhanced by frequent changes within New Testament scholarship' (140), as if individual New Testament scholars were somehow the measure of the meaning of its message. Such a belief would be very pretentious (though the academic community is often sorely tempted to hold it). It is just as plausible to argue that the differences between scholars have less to do with the application of a rigorous exegetical methodology than with the uncritical and unsophisticated naivety of regarding it 'as important to use [the] dominant philosophical ethos to interpret theology, even when aware that this ethos will be replaced by another' (137).

There is one further area of theological concern, which will lead us naturally to the final objection to the notion of religious pluralism: this is the emphasis on God as the creator and the lessening of the biblical witness to him as the saviour and liberator. The purpose behind this shift is the need to give a convincing theological explanation of how it is that followers of quite diverse beliefs manifestly fulfil the divine will.

God, it is said, belongs to all the nations. As the creator of every living being on the earth, God has not left himself without a witness as to his true nature and purposes for humankind. The doctrine of creation unites the whole human family. It asserts one common origin and the equality of our worth, whatever the circumstances into which we were born. The doctrine of salvation, however, divides, for in its Old Testament unveiling it assumes the election of one people from among all the peoples and in its New Testament statement it assumes that only one particular group of people (the Church) has access to God's saving grace in Jesus Christ. There is no statement more unacceptable to the religious pluralist than the ancient confession that, 'outside the Church there is no salvation'.

Nevertheless, in reality, the Christian claim that salvation can only be attained through the particular death Jesus died and through his resurrection on the third day is no more exclusive than the claims made about the way of salvation in Buddhism, Hinduism and Islam. In each of these perspectives the meaning of salvation is given in such a way that, if it were true, the other understandings would be excluded. In spite of what may appear on the surface, each religion, in order to maintain its own inner coherence and integrity, has to exclude the claims of the others. Choices have to be made.

We are indeed one at the point of our humanity. The way of being human is essentially the same, whatever may be the different cultural manifestations. This is not just theologically true, but biologically confirmed (we are all of one blood) and psychologically evident (the same kind of events cause us all to cry and to laugh). But at the point of our understanding of why we fail to be what we know we should be, there are fundamental disagreements. In other words, we agree substantially about what makes us human, but we profoundly dispute the way to overcome what is inhuman within us. We may be largely at one in describing our common humanity, but not in pointing to the path which leads to the new humanity.

It is in this context that we have to affirm that a consistent pluralism is quite incompatible with a prophetic witness and practice. In the prophetic message, as it has come to us in the Bible, no wedge can be driven between God the creator and God the redeemer. This is particularly clear in the second part of Isaiah. God has a controversy both with his own people and with all the nations that surround them. They have all chosen to go their own ways, rather than observe the terms of the covenant that God made with them. The consequence is that they do evil. Exploitation of the weak, violence against the poor, manipulation of the legal system against the defenceless is wrong.

It is a fundamental assumption of the prophetic message that the people's unrighteous acts flow from a wrong concept of God, and also end up in a wrong concept of God. So oppression in all its forms is fortified by recourse to false religion: 'As for the prophets who lead my people astray, if one feeds them, they proclaim "peace"; if he does not, they prepare to wage war against him . . . The seers will be ashamed and the diviners disgraced' (Mic. 3:5–7). But if religious pluralism were to be the correct way of looking at people's experience, there could be no prophetic voice of protest against human evil (we will explore the reasons for this in the next section). Nor would there be the prophetic message of comfort and hope that God has provided a way of liberation by laying on the servant whom he has chosen the iniquity of us all (Isa. 52:13–53:12).

The ethical dangers inherent in pluralism

Neither John Hick's concept of reality-centredness nor Wilfred Cantwell Smith's reinterpretation of faith can deal adequately with the question of inherent evil in the world. If there is no certain access to final truth, there is no knowing what might be mistaken and wrong. And if there is no way that error can be recognised with certainty, then evil could just as easily be another facet of ultimate reality as goodness, truth or beauty (as indeed it is in some, 'Manichean', religious philosophies). In other words, on the assumptions of the religious pluralists there can be no criteria for distinguishing between a benevolent and a malignant transcendence. This is an extremely serious consequence for those whose philosophical stance pushes them to defend a relativistic interpretation of the world.

In his critique of Cantwell Smith's use of the term faith, Harry Hoehler (1990) highlights the ethical dilemma which faces those who cannot bring themselves to make any direct and univocal identification between the content of belief and the act of faith. Smith's conviction that faith is the central and universal religious characteristic is pivotal to his desire to see a convergence of the world's religious traditions. But, asks Hoehler, among whom is there an identity of faith? Does one include thoroughly oppressive, racially bigoted ideologies like National Socialism and convictions like those held by the Ku-Klux-Klan? If not, on what grounds are they excluded, since each world-view incorporates Cantwell Smith's definition of faith, namely an orientation of personality to the transcendent?

Unfortunately for his position, in the world as it actually is there is no such thing as an innocent pursuit of the truth. If there is a radical disjunction between faith's focus and faith's response, then anything is legitimate. There can be little doubt that at different times and places some have found that the beliefs of Stalinism, fascism and apartheid have produced in their lives 'a transforming personal experience'. Faith then becomes an act of individual intensity and allegiance, equally valid in every situation. Such a conviction opens the way for any kind of religious or ideological fanaticism. Hoehler sums up the grave problem that such a pluralistic definition of faith entails in a pungent aphorism: if faith does not mean more than deep personal commitment, we are in deep trouble.

The characteristics of religion

It has been one of the main theses of this study that religion as such usually acts as a negative factor in human life. Therefore, religion is open to the secular criticism that it impedes and distorts the path to real human emancipation and freedom. Religion belongs essentially to a pre-modern phase of human development. It is simply unthinkable that the gains of a secular view of the world could be given up and that human communities could return to an acceptance of 'superstitious' beliefs, however sophisticated they are made to appear. For the moment, I accept these sentiments as largely valid (and will go on to explain why), though with the strong proviso that the secular consensus has brought with it irreparable losses as well as gains.

Religious beliefs and practices have arisen in an amazing variety of forms across the whole of human history. They seem to function to fulfil a number of deeply felt needs. It is a universally observable fact that people need to be able to make some sense of their own lives and the world they live in. They are constrained to respond to what we might call the most fundamental questions of existence: birth and death, human sexuality, success and failure, suffering, moral obligations, social position, the human differences of gender, race, language and culture, and many more. Religions have been powerful ways of attempting to answer the deeper mysteries of life. Where they have been in decline, people have been correspondingly more confused about these issues.

Increasingly in the Western world, there is a desire to escape from what Herbert Marcuse called a one-dimensional existence. There is an aspiration for something beyond the tedious round of trivial tasks, based on conformity to an apparently mechanistic universe which, in spite of our longing for something different, constrains our freedom. In a confusing, fragmented world, with a deep loss of family stability and sense of roots, many are searching for the source of their own personhood. In spite of the fact that a modern, irreligious culture proclaims that morality is a matter of private choice, and therefore each of us is free to choose the lifestyle which seems most appropriate, people still have to cope with seemingly illogical feelings of guilt and shame.

However, the fact that religion is designed to fulfil a number of functions does not make it necessarily right or true. It may simply be one more example of the way in which human beings tend to treat all things as a commodity. Though potentially able to unleash enormous hidden powers, religion is so often treated as something to be possessed and controlled in order that our lives may run smoothly and not be troubled by unforeseen, malignant forces. That is why most religions have a class of people considered to be the most expert interpreters of realities beyond our vision and comprehension. Because of their own training or experience, they are considered to be in some measure mediators between us and the powers beyond. That is also why, at a popular level, most religions are practised as a mixture of recognisably traditional beliefs and magical customs. There is a universal language of superstition, which varies little from one religious culture to another. There is also a common belief in the efficacy of specific practices like pilgrimages, fasting, personal sacrifices, attendance at particular rituals, the prayer of certain 'holy' people, and so on. In other words, religion depends on there being a radical divide between a sacred, mysterious, numinous or spiritual world and the unromantic ordinary experience of everyday life.

It is for this reason that consistent secularists insist that all religious convictions and desires are projections on to another, make-believe realm of existence, which the human being has created as an ideal world. They are wish-fulfilments which express the potent, universal desire that the actual state of affairs was different, that the experience of conflict and anguish could be resolved, or at least powerfully ameliorated.

Given that, according to secularist beliefs, the human race is alone in the universe, the search for meaning and comfort in another realm of existence is an illusion. The utopian dream, in whatever form it comes, is an inversion of reality, which diverts precious human energies away from the much more complex task of making the present world a better place for all to live in. In this sense, religion is harmful. Through education and the pressure of a culture emancipated from crude beliefs in the supernatural it should be actively countered.

From a Christian perspective also, but for subtly different reasons, all religion, in so far as it adopts a quasi-magical approach to existence, is harmful. For example, doctrines which are dependent in some measure on astrological forecasts or the discernment of omens or which posit a series of rebirths, according to the merit one may have gained or the punishment one may have deserved, deprive the human spirit of any genuine hope. They are fatalistic and, therefore, oppressive.

The functional view of religion, so popular in this age of relativism, has always depended historically on a correct approach to the collective traditions of the religious community with which one is identified, either by birth or choice. Personal harmony can only be guaranteed if a basic social cohesion is maintained. That is why it is so hard for people in deeply religious communities to change their faith commitment. Dependence on the agreed boundaries of belief within the community and the lack of any mechanism for challenging the consensus are also oppressive.

In treating religious life in this way, there is undoubtedly a danger of over-generalising. Have not all religions to some extent been able to escape from a magical world-view and a socially conformist structure? Indeed, they have. The generalisation is intended to provide a basic set of criteria by which one may distinguish between oppressive and liberating forces operating in the world. Wherever exceptions to the general description occur, and they do, there we may be able to find examples of God's liberating truth breaking into human existence.

However, it is only possible to maintain that the cumulative evidence of history points in the direction of the oppressive nature of religion (and indeed of some manifestations of secular thought and action), and to talk about exceptions, if there exists one message which is entirely exempt from the general criticisms of religion we have been making. Otherwise, there would be no sufficient basis on which to distinguish between religion as opium and liberation. Another main thesis of this book is that that one message is derived from the story of Jesus Christ. Such an assertion clearly needs to be tested.

Why Christianity is not a religion

Let me admit straightaway that trying to remove Christianity altogether from the general category of religion seems to demonstrate the very worst form of special pleading. In practice, without doubt, Christianity displays many of the same features as other religions – for example, structures, professionalisms, rituals, beliefs in the semi-magical efficacy of certain conventions and strategies. It would appear, therefore, that the attempt can only lead to some highly theoretical position without any real relevance to normal life. The discussion about religion, it will be said, is about the way ordinary people organise their convictions in concrete structures and practices. This is undeniable. Nevertheless, in the light of the central message of Jesus Christ many of these must be judged accretions which tend to distort, rather than interpret, the real substance of the faith. Unless the distinction can be made, not only in theory but also in the way the faith is lived, there would be no way of understanding what intrinsically belongs to the unalterable core and what does not. People of other beliefs must decide whether they too wish to dissociate themselves from the term religion, or whether they happily accept that they belong to what is termed a 'world religion'.

One argument for distinguishing between religion and Christianity has to do with the famous projection theory of religion (see chapter 2, 'Infantile helplessness'). There is a fundamental difference, both in the theory and practice of Christianity, between that which is desired and that which is the case. Thus, in the prophetic tradition there is a way of distinguishing between a true understanding of God and his ways and the message of the false prophets. It was the latter who were preaching what the people wanted to believe was the case, namely that God, as a reward for devotion to religious duties and in spite of what was happening to the powerless people of society, would always remain benevolent towards his people. The projection theory breaks down as an explanation as soon as it is possible to demonstrate that the object of faith demands the end of all comfortable illusions about religious practice.

The faith of the Bible is characterised by a fundamental rupture between the religious expectations of the people and the true, living God. It is, perhaps, still imaginable that the projection theory could account for belief in a divine being who demands both that we renounce all attempts to manipulate him for our own benefit and that we open ourselves to the unpredictable risk of being transformed root and branch from what we actually are. However, it is highly implausible that people would be so deliberately 'masochistic' if there were other less challenging beliefs to hand. People believe in this kind of God not because they see any immediate short-term, or even long-term benefit for themselves, but because this God actually is.

Jesus Christ in word and action proclaimed and demonstrated a total liberation from every oppressive feature of religion. This, even more than his particular concern for the poor and oppressed, or his critical and dismissive attitude towards the pretensions of political power, makes him the unique and radical figure that he is.

Or, perhaps, one ought to say that his basic compassionate concern for the poor (cf. Mt. 9:36; 14:14; 23:4; Lk. 14:21–4; Jn. 10:7–10) is that they should be liberated from the illusory claims of religion which hinder a genuine openness to the reality of God's transforming rule in the whole of life. Far and away the harshest condemnation is reserved for the religious professionals who have adapted beliefs to suit their own ends, and who seek to prevent the ordinary person from being transformed by the presence of God's Messiah in their midst. The kingdom of God represents a radical reorientation of one's whole being to God, allowing him alone the right to dictate the terms of the relationship.

Paul discovered this same truth in his Damascus road encounter with Jesus Christ crucified and risen from the dead. As he explains at different places in his occasional letters (e.g., Galatians and Philippians) his life was changed from its former religious orientation within that strand of

Jewish faith that he had embraced. His former problem was his excess of religious fervour. Now his new understanding that Jesus was the Messiah represented what one can only call a paradigm shift away from religion. He himself uses the imagery of being delivered from slavery so that he might enjoy the freedom of being a full member of the family (Gal. 4).

Paul had to step outside of the closed world of religion before he could understand the meaning of God's grace. Whatever his own particular psychological frame of mind, he found the true centre of a liberating faith when he became discontented with the practice of religion. He had to discover the oppressive nature of religion before he could understand the contrasting message of the gospel. Freedom in Christ is freedom from the kind of taboo which also kept the apostle Peter captive to notions of ritual and racial uncleanness.

For these reasons there is absolutely no question of Christianity being the highest, or a superior form of religion. When dealing with ultimate questions of grace and truth there is a qualitative difference between the message of Christ and anything else ever believed. Unless the core of the gospel message has been changed in its substance, it is a fact that the closer one gets to the centre of another faith the further one is from the Christian understanding of God as fully made known in the historical reality of Jesus Christ, and vice versa. Of course, there are parallels between religions, but the crucial issue does not concern their outward forms, nor even their agreement about some important ethical principles (also shared with non-religious people), but how these relate to the central self-understanding of the religion in question.

This is what makes all attempts to find some genuinely convergent substratum of transcendent or ultimate belief in all religions an illusory quest. Such a search, as has often been pointed out, ends up in general, abstract and vague affirmations, which most religious adherents cannot recognise as describing their convictions. One wonders why diffuse generalisations are considered a more appropriate approach to inter-faith dialogue than a recognition from the outset that incompatible and mutually exclusive beliefs have to be acknowledged and discussed. One honours the religious convictions and practices of another faith believer much more by working through the difficulties of living together without discrimination, when fundamental beliefs are not shared, than by pretending that all human beings are on the same pilgrimage together. Such an assumption is not only false, it is an affront to the integrity of other believers.

God at work among people of different faiths

It is significant how much of the debate about religious pluralism hinges on the credibility of experience. Hick begins from the assumption that diverse religious experiences and thoughts constitute different human perceptions of the divine or the ultimately real in itself, or of some metaphysical pressure on human consciousness. However, the claim of experience in itself, without any kind of verifiable external referent, is an intensely private affair. It could only be compared with other people's experiences if there were an accepted code by which the language in which the experience was communicated had a constant and generally recognised meaning. Otherwise the experience would remain locked within the individual's experience. It could not come out and be shared. Thus, there would be no way of knowing whether Hick's assumption was true or not. It is precisely the impossibility of finding an external referent to experience which commands general agreement that causes the religious pluralist's whole edifice to collapse like a house of cards.

As long as experience remains non-cognitive and symbolic, rather than cognitive and literal, there is no way of building a bridge between the claims and the reality. Experience, in other words, is no evidence that God is genuinely being touched. Different experiences only demonstrate that people give different interpretations to what they feel is happening to them. As T. R. Mathis (1985:ix) points out in his criticism of Hick, there is a fundamental incompatibility between his secular, empiricist base and the kind of theological superstructure he is trying to erect. One is bound to wonder whether the multi-faith, pluralist thesis is not a last-ditch attempt to produce a spiritual meaning for human existence out of a closed world-order. If so, it is a tragically lost cause!

A number of other tough problems exist in the way of accepting the general thesis that somehow all religious beliefs and practices manifest God at work. There is, for example, the diversity of belief. How is it possible to make any meaningful comparison between views as different as those of the Vedantic Hindu belief that all reality (including a supreme being) is one, and the rigorous understanding of the separation between God and human beings one finds in Islam? Or how does one put together the Jewish experience of suffering with Theravada Buddhism's rejection of the ultimate reality of suffering as part of *anicca*, existence without any abiding reality?

If one is going to speak of God manifest in other religions, it is necessary to be more precise. In which aspects of the various religious traditions has God manifested himself in a way which would not contradict claims made for the other traditions? The problem of generalising matches the impossibility of starting from a generic concept like religious experience. Unless there is a firm knowledge of who God is, to affirm his presence in other religions is a quite meaningless idea. It is not surprising, then, as Newbigin has pointed out (1988:317), that the '"God" who is at the centre of Hick's Copernican system is God as Hick has come to know him through the Christian tradition'.

Likewise, Cantwell Smith (1987:171) is bound to affirm that God *is*, as Christ has revealed him, 'a God of mercy and love . . . who delights to save'. He goes on to say that any other vision of God contradicts the central revelation of Christ, thereby implying that there can be false views of

God. That being so, where does the true understanding come from, if not from one particular disclosure of his nature and will? No pluralism here!

Another aspect of this question concerns the issue of credentials. Unless one does not discriminate at all between one set of beliefs and practices and another – and in practice it is impossible not to do so – it is necessary to ask by what criteria one discerns that God is at work. As Kenneth Cracknell says (1986:85), 'whatever path human beings choose is not necessarily a reflection of the way of God'.

There is a further question, not adequately dealt with by those who strongly advocate the reality of God among people of strong religious convictions: Why do we think that God's activity is more present among people of strictly religious belief than among those who do not consistently practise any kind of religious observance and yet who hold strongly to humane values in life? Behind this question lies a more fundamental one: On what basis should one take for granted the supposition that people of religious faith are more likely to touch the reality of God in the world than those who make no religious profession? Failure to take this question seriously has led to a devaluation of the positive aspects of a secular culture in its tacit repudiation of the many alienating, superstitious and immature elements in all religious beliefs.

Until the modern era, whatever may have been their practical and theoretical failures to understand and take God seriously, Christians have never doubted God's ability to communicate truly his nature and will to those he has created and called into fellowship with himself. From a Christian perspective the heart of the truth about God is that he has become a human being. This being so, Christians have to stress that the centrality of the personal and the particular in one's understanding of the divine reality is non-negotiable.

Other views, which to be true to themselves are bound to deny this insistence on the mediation of God's being through this or other specific moments of space and time, are not complementary understandings of the divine, they are false. The test of this comes, not at the periphery of what Christians have always and everywhere held to be true, but at the very heart of their faith. The heart of God is supremely and finally manifested in Jesus' cry of dereliction on the cross. Yet, the suffering of God in the pain and sin of humankind as it is borne by Jesus Christ is a notion universally rejected by all other faiths. How, then, does one suppose that they manifest something of the truth of God? If God is truly at work, revealing himself as he is among people of religious faith, why do they not readily recognise that God was *in Christ* reconciling the world to himself? To talk in general terms about God's presence may be sheer sentimentality, unless one is willing to deal with the hard questions about his particularity.

The question of the criteria of discernment we will leave until the final section of this chapter. However, in the light of the overall experience of religion down the ages, it is a fair assessment of real life to say that religious experience and commitment can make no prior claim to be a privileged vehicle for grasping the truth of God and the universe he has created. The fact that God has not left himself without a witness is indeed attested in the many perceptions of and commitment to what is good, just, liberating and wholesome. But this grasp of the ultimate nature of reality has often happened as a struggle against religious beliefs and practices, or in spite of them.

In one sense, it does not matter too much whether the theological explanation for the ability of human beings to touch the reality of God in the world comes through the doctrine of creation (human beings are equally and inescapably in the image of God), or through a Christological approach (the Word manifested in flesh and blood is also the light of the world, which allows everyone glimpses of ultimate truth), or through a doctrine of the Spirit, sent to convict the world of right and wrong and the necessity of judgement. What does matter is that religious and non-religious life may equally well both manifest aspects of this truth and distort and suppress it. There are no grounds for special claims, save in the one case of Jesus Christ.

Thus, from the Christian point of view I am advocating, not only did Muhammad, in many ways, have a true perception of God, even if partial and one-sided (he appears too much as 'God, the Conqueror', whereas in truth God is more 'fully human' than the Qur'an allows), so did Karl Marx, even if it was expressed in terms of a denial. In the case of the latter, God could not be like the supreme being of bourgeois Christianity, who sanctioned a human community divided into classes and in which money reigned as the final arbiter of good and evil.

One is forced by the logic of the argument, and the reality of ordinary life on the ground, to come to the uncomfortable but absolutely unavoidable conclusion that religious beliefs and observances (including those held and practised on many occasions by Christians) are by no means necessarily the right criteria for asking questions about God's activity in human life. God is just as likely (more likely, probably, in the light of the biblical tradition of Israel and the temple) to be absent from religion. If it is true that the only full account that we have of God is in the human life of Jesus, the Christ, then we are bound to conclude that we recognise God at work, not in religious experiences, rites, customs and values, but in the liberating anticipations of his future kingdom which are visible now among people, whether religious or not.

The meaning of Jesus Christ is the meaning of Christian faith

It may well be because of the absolute particularity of Jesus of Nazareth and the inescapable challenge of his life to every human idea and venture that both the accounts of his mission in first-century Palestine and their interpretation have been a battlefield of conflicting views.

It is axiomatic to the whole thesis of this book that we must be able to have a reliable account of his actions and teaching. If there is any hint that the details of Jesus Christ's ministry are not recoverable, or that they are open to many divergent, and even contradictory, interpretations, each of which, given the nature of the evidence, is equally valid, then the critical content of the message about him has irretrievably slipped from view. From now on Christ can be moulded and manipulated according to a thousand different options. Our religions and ideologies are in control, and the truth is bent and made to fit whatever exciting new idea or scheme happens to appeal to us.

It would be foolish to pretend to be able to rehearse all the critical arguments used in the last two hundred years to discredit the accuracy of the gospel accounts of Jesus. It is sufficient for the present to point out that the methods of historical investigation used have often been highly problematical. In many cases, for example, contemporary philosophical prejudices have been allowed to dictate the kind of reconstruction of the historical Jesus regarded as authentic. An alien framework of interpretation (for example, belief in a closed-universe system, or radical political self-righteousness) has been imposed upon the text. This is an oppressive approach, for it violates the integrity of the text and curtails its freedom to speak its own message. It would be much more honest to disagree openly with it, than to pretend that it really says something else.

The refusal to allow the text to be taken at face value, and the *a priori* conviction that the writers' or their communities' own faith has produced interpretations of Jesus which make the true events irrecoverable, has led to explanations which are circular in their reasoning and implausible in their conclusions. It is assumed that the early Christian communities developed their understanding of the meaning of Jesus in response to a number of different problems and crises which confronted them in the turbulent years in Palestine leading up to the Jewish war of AD 66–70, not least in their own self-understanding over against the various parties within Judaism. This development is then discovered within the gospel portraits of Jesus.

In this way, despite the lack of corroborative evidence from outside the Gospels, the thesis, which was assumed only as a possible hypothesis, has been discovered to be true: what we have in the gospel records is an inextricable mixture of real happenings in the life of Jesus and of the faith which evolved in the early Church. Thus, sayings about divorce, or the paying of taxes or the destruction of Jerusalem, or many others, are not what Jesus actually said in his own context, but what he might have said had he been living within those early Christian communities.

One aspect of this way of proceeding, which has undeniably important consequences for the debate about Jesus Christ and the religions, is the question about Jesus' consciousness of his own divine nature. One strong tradition, which surfaces time and again in many of the discussions on inter-faith matters, asserts that Jesus *became* the Son of God in the course of his faithful fulfilment of the mission to which he was committed. By his openness to and spiritual unity with the will of the Father he showed himself to be in a very special relationship to God. By his option for the poor and his prophetic denunciation of an oppressive religious and political regime he proved himself to be the supreme paradigm of filial obedience to the loving stance of God towards the weak and vulnerable. By his ultimate self-sacrifice for the sake of truth and justice he demonstrated an ultimate freedom in serving God's purposes, which was rewarded by being designated Son of God through the resurrection.

This way of reading the Gospels (technically known as an adoptionist Christology) has, for some people, several advantages. For example, it allows those who are embarrassed by the ontological language of the traditional ways of understanding the relationship of the Son and the Father to adopt functionalist language which seems much more in tune with the intellectual mood of modern times. Yet, at the same time, Jesus is accorded a very high (maybe even a unique) place in the fulfilment of God's plans of salvation.

More important, however, it does not set Jesus wholly

apart from other religious leaders of other traditions and histories. Though one may be able to claim for him a certain uniqueness in the sense that he has gone further than any other human being in the perfection of his unqualified love for God and for suffering humanity, that uniqueness does not spring from who he always was, but from what he did. Other religious figures likewise, though not to the same intensity, have been open to God and have given themselves unstintedly to the poor and needy. An adoptionist Christology of this kind also fits harmoniously into the general religious category of merit. Jesus can be seen as a religious figure who did well and was rewarded.

Such an approach to the Jesus of history is intended to take history seriously by rescuing a so-called kernel from a so-called husk. It allows us to go from the particular to the universal, rather than starting (as is supposed in traditional Christologies) from arbitrary universals: for example, that Jesus was already fully God in the womb of his mother, in the temple at the age of twelve, and when he came into Galilee preaching the kingdom of God.

Adoptionist Christology is said to be chronologically the most primitive form, reflecting the earliest belief of the Christian community. Therefore, where in the gospel accounts of Jesus he is presented as pre-existent, eternal and ontologically one with the Father (most notably in John's Gospel), these affirmations are reputed to be part of the Church's confession at a much later stage of its developing understanding of Jesus. In the actual historical life of Jesus they are clearly anachronistic.

This way of driving a wedge between Jesus' own self-understanding and the dogmatic faith of his later followers is ingenious and rests on a good deal of sophisticated investigation of the gospel texts. Nevertheless, it is based, unhappily, on a flawed methodological procedure in which the final conclusion (Jesus did not think of himself as God) is already contained in the initial, *a priori* assumption (it must be possible to trace in the history of the first Christian communities the evolution of a set of convictions about

Jesus which move from a lower to a higher form). Such a method cannot take the text seriously as it stands, for it already knows what the text means, whatever may appear to the contrary. And it is what it means, not what it says, which is decisive for the investigative process. Ultimately, then, much historical-critical work on the Gospels constitutes a (religious) manipulation of Jesus, by which he is squeezed into categories of the interpreter's own making.

With regard to this so-called critical approach to the Gospels, it is interesting to note that in many instances theory and practice are far apart. That is to say, the way in which the authority of the life and teaching of Jesus is translated polemically into the realm of inter-faith dialogue or political commitments does not match the historical probability, which is said to derive from careful critical analysis.

What tends to happen is that the real Jesus is distinguished from inauthentic accretions, according to what is demanded by the particular stance being taken. Thus, if a particular aspect of Jesus' ministry seems to provide evidence which goes counter to the ideological or faith position being taken, it is automatically assigned to the faith of the early Church and dismissed as irrelevant to our knowledge of Jesus himself.

From this whole discussion I would like to draw three fundamental conclusions. Each one, in its own way, has crucial implications for the question: By what criteria do we know the truth about God?

Firstly, *Jesus Christ is not retranslatable*. The text must be treated as it stands, with full integrity. In the first instance it does not mean anything else than what it says, according to normal grammatical rules, the significance of the vocabulary used, properly identifiable literary conventions, and the overall historical, cultural and linguistic context in which it has been written. In other words, the true meaning is the natural meaning.

The implications of this view are at least threefold: the text itself, rather than any *a priori* considerations, determines the message we receive from it; we are not at liberty to decide on some other basis, apart from the text, what is to be received as authentically from Jesus; Jesus is as he is in the text, taking every story and didactic passage as of decisive evidence for a full picture of his person and achievement. One of the reasons why there have been so many 'Jesuses' abstracted from the New Testament in the last 150 years is precisely because, in the interests of some cause or other, only that part of the whole which fits the picture has been allowed as evidence for the historical Jesus. Never, perhaps, in the whole history of historical criticism have documents been so subjected to such an arbitrary process.

Secondly, *the appearance is the reality*. If we are right in believing that there is no viable alternative to accepting that there is, in the recorded life of Jesus, a complete coincidence between what is portrayed and what is the case, then we need to handle all use of the language of symbol and myth with extreme caution. Symbolism is a dramatic literary device for communicating a literal reality in a non-literal, figurative fashion. It is one of a rich diversity of ways of expressing what is. Its power lies in its ability to explore depths of meaning through the use of imagination. But the meaning, though accessible to us through a different form, nevertheless coincides with the reality which lies behind. In its consistently biblical usage the symbol is never a metaphor for what our philosophical assumptions do not allow us to define.

Thirdly, and this is the necessary consequence of all that has been affirmed so far, *Jesus Christ belongs to no one*. The only way that Jesus, and the message about him, can be delivered from the domesticating effect of religious and ideological presuppositions is by accepting that the given text is the final benchmark for distinguishing between the reality about him and imaginative supposition. Of course, as a starting-point for distinguishing between true belief and action and the immense variety of ideas which stem from wish-fulfilment, it is a matter of faith rather than incontrovertible proof. But then so also, and with much less rational basis, is the position which finds such a claim intolerable.

Why should people find the thesis that the truth about God has been given in the form of propositions about Jesus Christ so unacceptable, even scandalous? Is it not because in this way the full force of the offence of Jesus to the religious spirit within the human heart is unavoidable? If we cannot reinterpret the text to make it conform to a different world-view, *we* are no longer in control. Our religious defences, behind which in one way or another we seek to hide from the living God, are torn down and strewn about us.

Jesus Christ as he was, and is, will always remain a scandal to the religious (and secularly religious) mind which believes it must maintain ownership over the traditions within which it has found its home. Like the best of homes, religious and non-religious faith gives a measure of comfort and security. To be confronted by the claims of the Christ, over whom one has no control, while one remains within the security of the home, is to induce the ultimate human crisis, the fear of the loss of identity. Hence, the passion with which control of the text is fought for.

One of the favourite phrases used in inter-faith dialogue is the expression, 'the search for God'. It is our search, in the sense that we ultimately are in control of the expedition and can decide when we have reached the desired destination, which is the discovery of a divine being with whom we 'feel comfortable'. It is similar to the venture by which the Europeans, who 'discovered' the Americas, Australia and Africa, settled down and made their homes, using the lands as they desired.

How different is the saying of Jesus, 'You did not choose me, but I chose you and appointed you to go and bear fruit' (Jn. 15:16). Here the initiative and the control are with Jesus. Only as *we* abandon the search for God can God find us in the one way he has ordained, through his servant Jesus. The truth of God can only be recognised in the act of it possessing and controlling our lives, directing us to go into the world as God has sent his Son into the world.

The search for truth is a contradiction in terms, for what

is found is possessed (I conquer, therefore I am); but that which finds us possesses us. God comes to us in so far as we abandon the religious, or other, traditions which keep us from having to cast ourselves entirely upon his mercy and grace. Blessed are the religiously poor.

One of the greatest tragedies of the Christian faith, and one of the main reasons why it has failed to make a greater impact on the world, is its pretension to *possess* the truth about Jesus and God. In the time-honoured way of religion, the call to follow Jesus has been converted into the false claim that he belongs to our community. There are 'orthodox' as well as relativistic ways of domesticating Jesus, and the Christian religion has become one of the most effective defences against the claims of Jesus to be the one and only rightful Lord: 'You call me "Teacher" and "Lord", and rightly so, for that is what I am . . . No servant is greater than his master, nor is a messenger greater than the one who sent him' (Jn. 13:13–16).

Signs of authenticity and liberation

The context of the debate we have been engaging in is immense. We are coming to the climax of it. Much of it has had to be cast in the form of critique, because so many of the assumptions which have led to the relativistic and pluralistic beliefs of our culture are no longer seriously questioned. They are taken as the self-evident truths of an emancipated world. We have sought to demonstrate that they are both impossible to believe and, when operative in the real world, oppressive in their results.

To outline positively some of the criteria by which we may test our knowledge of the truth about God, the universe and our existence runs the risk of being inadequate and simplistic. There is no alternative, however, for much of the argument of this book has hinged on the affirmation that final truth is not so much a goal to be discovered at another time and in another place, as a given reality, already existing close at hand (cf. Rom. 10:6–9), to be believed and obeyed.

There is only one place where we can begin: the claim by Jesus Christ that he is the truth, and his affirmation that God's word, which he hears and proclaims without distortion, is also truth. The claim assumes that everything else which directly or indirectly claims to be true must be measured and judged against this one prior assertion. To authenticate this massive claim, one might look at some of the following criteria.

Firstly, the affirmation must be consistent within itself. A lack of internal consistency, while in certain exceptional cases it may have an adequate explanation, damages the credibility of what is being said.

Secondly, there must be a coherence with the totality of the reality which human beings always and everywhere have experienced in their lives. Truth is only true if it is able to deal adequately with all the fundamental questions of life and with all human needs. Because the truth which has been given is not exhaustive, in certain areas we may only be able to come to provisional answers. There are undoubtedly some very deep questions (for example, about the ultimate nature of God, about the existence of innocent suffering, about free-will) for which now there are no wholly comprehensive answers. Nevertheless, one may argue that what is already knowable from revelation already gives a more adequate explanation than current alternatives. The other side of the argument from coherence is that the truth as proclaimed must be able to show why other, alternative claims are deficient.

A third important criterion is one we have already touched on many times. It must be possible to show that all the reasons given for holding that the truth claim about what is the case is merely the projection of an inner desire fail to provide a comprehensive explanation. In this way the very serious accusations that faith alienates people from their real humanity, or manifests a failure of nerve to create a more noble species, or keeps people in a position of servile dependence on a father-figure – made in the name of Marx,

Nietzsche, Freud and many others – must be shown to be ultimately inadequate.

The final and most important criterion is that the claims made should result in the genuine liberation of the human being and human community. This accords with the inseparable relationship between truth and liberation which Jesus himself has drawn, 'the truth will set you free' (Jn. 8:32). Naturally, to make the equation, we have to know what it means to be free. Here, the additional claim of Jesus Christ, 'I am . . . the life' (Jn. 14:6), comes into play. Liberation is release from every attitude and conduct which is contradicted by the life of Jesus. It is to be free of all that damages and restrains the possibility of human beings becoming fully human *in the image of Jesus*. Perhaps the greatest examples in our contemporary world of people who are genuinely liberated by the Spirit of Christ are those who have deliberately faced the possibility of death, or at least have accepted a life of considerable deprivation, in order to demonstrate to abandoned and exploited peoples the reality of Jesus' sacrifice and conquest of death on their behalf. They are those who, in the words of the Book of Revelation, 'did not love their lives so much as to shrink from death' (Rev. 12:11). They show in a concrete way that, for the sake of others, they have already been freed from the supreme fear. That is liberation indeed!

Liberation is not necessarily the same as current notions of freedom, particularly if these are defined in terms of the autonomy of individual humans: each person outside the control of any external referent which compels belief or action. As is often pointed out, the kind of freedom which believes it possible to reject all authorities other than those freely chosen is a will-o'-the-wisp.

It is impossible to come to a place and a time where one is able to take off and throw away, like discarded, worn-out clothes, every imaginable influence on our lives, so that, at last we can stand naked and choose now, wholly for ourselves, which clothes we will wear. Already we will have on, like underwear invisible to us, some system of belief (probably one relatively fashionable within the culture) which is already determining our choice. Indeed, the very notion that one can be free from the authority of alien traditions is itself just such a system of belief.

In Christian terms it is not possible to reject God, in order to live in the freedom of a world without God, without having already accepted another god. It is perfectly possible to live on the basis that no personal God, creator of the universe, exists. What is not possible is to live as if there was no authority over our lives. A little careful thought would reveal that even the two most extreme forms of anti-authoritarianism, anarchy (without authority) and libertarianism, exercise their own form of debilitating control. There is no escape within human existence from this fact.

Over and over again, with extreme realism, the biblical message calls the attempted flight from God's authority idolatry (bending the knee at another shrine). It warns that the inevitable consequence is a self-chosen bondage; for whatever god is chosen, it does not have the power to make us more human. Only God can do that, through Jesus, for he alone knows what he has created, why it has gone wrong, and how it may be repaired.

Let us take one instance of this. As we have seen, at the centre of the message of Jesus Christ is the reality of truth and grace. To be fully human is to live by and for grace. Grace assumes that life must be lived as a constant thanksgiving, receiving in dependence a gift which it is not in our power to give ourselves. It is the gift of forgiveness, in which the awesome power of wrong and evil is broken and its destructive consequences annulled.

Grace contradicts the religious spirit, whether in its traditional form of seeking to atone for wrong-doing, prevail against disaster or gain God's favour in some way, or in its modern, secular form of the self-confident belief that the human self has sufficient resources to fulfil its destiny. So, one can choose to live by grace, including the grace of extending unmerited forgiveness and commitment to others, or one can live religiously. There is no third option. Grace, however, is dependent upon Jesus' unstinted offering of himself to his Father in thanksgiving for the Father's unswerving compassion for a humanity which refuses to be free.

Liberation, which is the ultimate criterion of truth, is a reality on the basis of that one supreme sacrifice which was the death of Jesus on a Roman cross. It was of such a nature that only God could offer it to God. The one and only wholly free person submitted himself to the bondage of evil and death in such a way that, in union with him, we could be free from all destructive forces. That same liberation is then worked in and through every aspect of our lives, and out into the institutions and customs of society, in such a way that we become committed from the heart to overcoming, wherever we can, the destructive force of sin.

Truth, which issues in liberation ('the truth will set you free', Jn. 8:32), is something which grasps hold of us and transforms us from being people who want to hold on to their lives to those who discover the purpose of their being in unselfishly giving up their lives for Jesus and his new creation. We may recognise truth, then, when we observe people living out lives of thanksgiving for the amazing grace of God in Jesus Christ. This grace has rescued us from the destructive consequences of our idolatry and selfishness and caused us to begin to live gladly in such a way that others too may experience liberation.

In the context of the encounter between people of different religions, we may accept the Copernican revolution of putting God at the centre of the universe of faiths, *as long as* he is the one and only God who has shown us his nature and purpose through the grace and liberating power of Jesus. But, in this we move away from the notion that inner experience can be the touchstone of truth to the manifest, concrete reality of a human life that can be touched, observed and listened to.

In the light of these criteria, we cannot say *a priori* that God is at work in all religions. In so far as they manifest elements of truth, grace and liberation in the sense defined by the life, death and resurrection of Jesus Christ, God's presence is definitive. They are, by definition, touching the reality of God himself. However, it may be more helpful to speak of the action of God in the lives of human beings, whether they identify with a formal religion or not. Sometimes there will be elements within the beliefs and practices by which they live which are full of grace and truth. The verdict of history, however, must be that religious commitment has more often than not caused people to live in the bondage of fear, fatalism, self-righteousness, fanaticism, aggression, superstition, authoritarianism and meritorious good deeds – the list could be extended. The first step on the path to becoming more truly human in the image of Jesus is, therefore, to renounce religion.

Discipleship in practice

It may well be that the emphasis of recent decades on dialogue between people of different religious convictions has to give way to a new consciousness among those who uphold a religious way of viewing the world. If my analysis has any substance in it, then what is needed is not so much a mutually supportive inter-faith discussion, based on the assumption that different religions represent different perspectives on the same basic truth, as an intra-faith consultation, prepared at least to consider the evidence that religions are the cause, not the solution, of many human problems.

One of the problematical elements in much inter-faith discussion is the assumption that religious life and values are of necessity a positive factor in human community. Such a starting-point tends to bracket out the crucial questions about truth and error, liberation and oppression, as being too divisive. How, though, are religious communities to be delivered, in the process of dialogue, from defensiveness, self-justification, even triumphalism?

The classical and well-rehearsed affirmation that there is 'no other name' by which liberation is possible, except that of Jesus, is not only an intellectual claim to be believed as objectively correct, but a call to follow Jesus in the way of liberation which he alone has opened up. The message of Jesus makes it quite clear that not only what is believed, but the way it is believed, is of supreme importance. Failure to recognise the unbreakable link between faith and practice has been one of the major reasons why Christian communities have so easily slipped into being the bastion of yet another religion or another sect.

The New Testament's confession of Christ must be believed in its entirety, not principally because it is a beautiful intellectual system, but because the whole reality of which it speaks is a liberating force, which restores humanity to the full dignity God intends for it. If it were not there, the human race would remain in ignorance and bondage.

The means which the Christian community uses to fulfil its mission are themselves part of the message. That is why the way Christians relate to those who do not share their belief in the gospel is itself either a confirmation or a denial of the truth, grace and liberation at the heart of its call to belong to Christ.

Faithfully following the way of Jesus seems to imply a number of consequences for authentic ways of relating to these other people. Presenting them will be an apt way of closing this whole discussion.

Firstly, the Christian relates from a place of weakness. The power of God at work in a believer to produce conviction about the truth of Jesus is wholly different from the power of an organisation or institution to use privilege, material incentives, sanctions or coercion to induce conversions. It is as different, say, as the father who gives his son money to travel, knowing that he will probably squander the gift in trivial pursuits, and the priest who threatens to evict a peasant from church land unless he is baptised.

Secondly, the Christian can only relate truly by listening attentively to all that the other person wants to communicate. The art of listening, particularly if the conversation proves to be critical of the Christian's stance, is painfully difficult for those who feel compelled, by the sheer wonder of the message they have been enabled to receive, to share it with others. But listening and understanding show that one believes in the absolute worth of the other person. Listening to criticism shows that one believes in the reality of sin and error and the need for forgiveness and healing.

Thirdly, the Christian relates by boldly (though not aggressively) stating and arguing the truth of Jesus as she or he has received it. Of course, this must be done in a way which is appropriate to each circumstance and sensitive to the need to build a long-lasting relationship, even when commitment to Christ is refused.

The message that in Jesus the bondage of a religious way of viewing the world is overcome is denied unless an invitation is extended to the other to be liberated by Christ and to become part of that community of disciples which is committed to his liberating message and action.

It is unrealistic to imagine that people can be fully liberated if they have never heard of the great and marvellous deeds that God, through Christ, has done for them. Anonymous Christianity leads to anonymous liberation. Evangelism, therefore, is an inescapable task. Its aim is not to expand denominations, but to bring together everywhere groups of people freed from the pain and disillusion of religious commitment, – by the Spirit of Jesus, who has been sent to make real in every situation Jesus' healing power (cf. Jn. 6:63; Rom. 8:13; 12:2; Gal. 5:22–5; Tit. 3:5–6) – to live henceforth on the basis of grace and truth.

Bibliography

The amount of books written in the general area of comparative beliefs, inter-faith dialogue and Christian attitudes to the many aspects of religious life is quite phenomenal. Needless to say, I have had time to peruse only a very small – though I hope representative – selection of them. The following list (which includes some unpublished papers) comprises books and articles which I have referred to in the text or consulted in an attempt to be better informed of the wide range of opinions and viewpoints about undoubtedly sensitive, controversial and emotionally intense subjects.

Ahmad, K., 1976. *Islam: Its Meaning and Message*. Leicester: The Islamic Foundation.

Ahmed, A., 1988. *Discovering Islam: Making Sense of Muslim History and Society*. London: Routledge & Kegan Paul.

Anderson, G., and T. Stransky, 1981a. *Christ's Lordship and Religious Pluralism*. Maryknoll, NY: Orbis Books.

Anderson, G., and T. Stransky, 1981b. *Mission Trends No. 5: Faith Meets Faith*. Grand Rapids, MI: Eerdmans.

Anderson, N., 1984. *Christianity and World Religions: The Challenge of Pluralism*. Leicester: IVP.

Ariarajah, W., 1988. *The Bible and People of Other Faiths*. Geneva: WCC.

Arles, S., 1988. 'Hindu Response to Pluralism', *Evangelical Review of Theology* 12.3.

Badham, P., ed., 1987. *Religion, State and Society in Modern Britain*. London: Macmillan.

Bailey, E., ed., *Aspects of Implicit and Civil Religion: A Selection of Readings and References with Introductions and Bibliographical Index*, 2 vols. Published by the author.

Bailey, E., ed., 1983. 'The Implicit Religion of Contemporary Society: An Orientation and Plea for its Study', *Religion* 13.1.

Bailey, E., 1985a. 'Civil Religion in Britain', in H. Kleger and A. Muller-Herold, eds., *Wertekonsens als Zivil-religion*. Munchen: Kaiser Verlag.

Bailey, E., 1985b. 'Implicit Religion and the Church'. Unpublished paper.

Bailey, E., 1986a. 'The Sacred Faith of the People', in A. Moss, ed., *In Search of Christianity*. London: Firethorn.

Bailey, E., ed., 1986b. *A Workbook in Popular Religion*. Dorchester: Partners Publications.

Bellah, R., 1969. 'Civil Religion in America', in D. Cutler, ed., *The World Year Book of Religion*. London: Evans Bros.

Bishop, P., 1979. *Words in World Religions*. London: SCM Press.

Boff, L., 1986. *Ecclesiogenesis: The Base Communities Reinvent the Church*. London: Collins.

Bowen, D., ed., 1981. *Hinduism in England*. Bradford: Bradford College.

Bowen, R., 1987. 'Inter-Faith Dialogue or Inter-Human Encounter?' *Anvil* 4.2.

Bowker, J., 1970. *Problems of Suffering in the Religions of the World*. Cambridge: Cambridge University Press.

Bowker, J., 1978. *Religious Imagination and the Sense of God*. Oxford: Clarendon Press.

Bowker, J., 1983. *Worlds of Faith*. London: BBC Books.

Bowker, J., 1987. *Licensed Insanity: Religions and Belief in God in the Contemporary World*. London: Darton, Longman & Todd.

Brown, J., 1980. *Men and Gods in a Changing World*. London: SCM Press.

Bruce, F. F., 1964. *The Epistle to the Hebrews*. Grand Rapids, MI: Eerdmans.

Camara, H., 1979. *The Conversions of a Bishop*. London: Collins.

Camps, A., 1983. *Partners in Dialogue: Christianity and Other World Religions*. Maryknoll, NY: Orbis Books.

Cantwell Smith, W., 1965. *The Faith of Other Men*. New York: Mentor Books.

Cantwell Smith, W., 1978. *The Meaning and End of Religion*. London: SCM Press.

Cantwell Smith, W., 1987. *Towards a World Theology: Faith and the Comparative History of Religion*. London: Macmillan.

Clarke, P., 1982. *West Africa and Islam*. London: Edward Arnold.

Clifton, R., 1986. 'The Popular Religion of a Country Area', in E. Bailey, ed., *A Workbook in Popular Religion*. Dorchester: Partners Publications.

Constantelos, D., 1981. 'Models for Christian Discipleship Amid Religious Pluralism: An Orthodox Perspective', in G. Anderson and T. Stransky, *Christ's Lordship and Religious Pluralism*. Maryknoll, NY: Orbis Books.

Copleston, F., 1982. *Religion and the One: Philosophies East and West*. Tunbridge Wells: Search Press.

Cotterell, P., 'Christianity and World Religions'. Unpublished paper.

Cracknell, K., 1986. *Towards a New Relationship: Christians and People of Other Faiths*. London: Epworth Press.

Cracknell, K., 'Faithfulness in an Age of Religious Pluralism'. Unpublished paper.

Cracknell, K., and C. Lamb, 1986. *Theology on Full Alert*. London: BCC.

Cragg, K., 1986. *The Christ and the Faiths: Theology in Cross-Reference*. London: SPCK.

Davie, G., 'The Nature of Belief in the Inner City'. Unpublished paper.

D'Costa, G., 1986. *Theology and Religious Pluralism*. Oxford: Blackwell.

D'Costa, G., ed., 1990. *The Myth of Christian Uniqueness Reconsidered*. Maryknoll, NY: Orbis Books.

Devasahayan, V., 'Pollution, Poverty and Powerlessness: A Dalit Perspective'. Unpublished paper.

Douglas, M., 1973. *Natural Symbols: Explorations in Cosmology*. Harmondsworth: Penguin Books.

Douglas, M., 1990. *Implicit Meanings: Essays in Anthropology*. London: Routledge.

Duchrow, U., and G. Liedke, 1989. *Shalom: Biblical Perspectives on Creation, Justice and Peace*. Geneva: WCC.

Dunn, J., and J. Mackey, 1987. *New Testament Theology in Dialogue*. London: SPCK.

Eliade, M., 1974. *From Primitives to Zen*. New York: Harper & Row.

Ellis, M., 1987. *Towards a Jewish Theology of Liberation*. Maryknoll, NY: Orbis Books.

Feuerbach, L., 1957. *The Essence of Christianity*. New York: Harper & Row.

Freud, S., 1973. *Introductory Lectures on Psychoanalysis*. Harmondsworth: Penguin Books.

Freud, S., 1985. *Origins of Religion: Totem and Taboo; Moses and Monotheism*. Harmondsworth: Penguin Books.

Freud, S., 1986. *Essentials of Psychoanalysis*. Harmondsworth: Penguin Books.

Gatting, M., 1989. *Leading from the Front*. London: Queen Anne Press.

Gill, R., 1989. *Competing Convictions*. London: SCM Press.

Gnanakan, K., 1989. *Kingdom Concerns*. Bangalore: Theological Book Trust.

Goddard, H., 1987. 'The Muslim Critique of the West', *Anvil* 4.2.

Goldmann, N., 1978. *The Jewish Paradox*. London: Weidenfeld & Nicolson.

Greely, A., *The Persistence of Religion*. London: SCM Press.

Griffiths, B., 1982. *The Marriage of East and West*. London: Collins.

Guinness, O., 1983. *The Gravedigger File*. London: Hodder & Stoughton.

Habgood, J., 1983. *Church and Nation in a Secular Age*. London: Darton, Longman & Todd.

Habib, G., 1987. 'Misuse of Religious Sentiments: Religion in Conflict Situations', in *Religious Liberty*. Geneva: WCC.

Hebblethwaite, B., 1987. 'Religious Language and Religious Pluralism', *Anvil* 4.2.

Hardy, T., 1978. *Tess of the D'Urbervilles*: Harmondsworth: Penguin Books.

Heim, E., 1985. *Is Christ the Only Way?* Valley Forge, NY: Judson Press.

Hemer, C., 1989. *The Book of Acts in the Setting of Hellenistic History*. Tubingen: Mohr.

Hick, J., 1977. 'The Copernican Revolution in Theology', in *God and the Universe of Faiths*. London: Collins.

Hick, J., 1980. *God Has Many Names*. London: Macmillan.

Hick, J., 1985. *Problems of Religious Pluralism*. London: Macmillan.

Hick, J., and B. Hebblethwaite, eds., 1980. *Christianity and Other Religions: Selected Readings*. London: Collins.

Hick, J., and P. Knitter, eds., 1987. *The Myth of Christian Uniqueness: Toward a Pluralistic Theology of Religions*. Maryknoll, NY: Orbis Books.

Hinnells, J., ed., 1985. *The Penguin Dictionary of Religions*. Harmondsworth: Penguin Books.

Hinnells, J., and E. Sharpe, 1972. *Hinduism*. London: Oriel Press.

Hoehler, H., 1990. 'Faith in the Thought of Wilfred Cantwell Smith', *Andover Newton Review* 1.1.

Hooker, R., 1989. *Themes in Hinduism and Christianity*. Frankfurt: Peter Lang.

Hooker, R., 'CMS and Other Faiths: Some Lessons from our History'. Unpublished paper.

Hornsby-Smith, M., 1986. 'Some Aspects of Popular Catholicism', in E. Bailey, ed., *A Workbook in Popular Religion*. Dorchester: Partners Publications.

Hughes, D., 1984. 'Christianity and Other Religions: A Review of Some Recent Discussion', *Themelios* 9.2.

Ikenga, E., 1983. 'Search for Methodology of African Religion', *West African Religion* 20.1/2.

Isbister, J., 1985. *Freud: An Introduction to His Life and Work*. Cambridge: Polity Press.

James, W., 1960. *The Varieties of Religious Experience: A Study in Human Nature*, introduced by A. D. Nock. London: Collins.

Jathana, C. D., ed., 1982. *Dialogue in Community*. Mangalore.

Jesudoss, D., 1986. *What is Man?* Madras.

Kateregga, B., and D. Shenk, 1981. *Islam and Christianity: A Muslim and Christian in Dialogue*. Grand Rapids, MI: Eerdmans.

Keddie, N. 1981. *Roots of Revolution: An Interpretive History of Modern Iran*. New Haven, NY: Yale University Press.

Kee, A., 1990. *Marx and the Failure of Liberation Theology*. London: SCM Press.

Keppel, G., 1985. *The Prophet and the Pharaoh: Muslim Extremism in Egypt*. London: Al Saqi Books.

Kim, Yong-Bock, 1990. 'The Mission of God in the Context of the Suffering and Struggling Peoples of Asia', in *Peoples of Asia, People of God*. Osaka: CCA.

King, U., 1986. *Seeing the Divine in Hinduism and Christianity*. Canterbury: The University Press.

Kings, G., 1987. 'Facing Mount Kenya: Reflections on the Bible and African Traditional Religion', *Anvil* 4.2.

Kirk, J. A., 1979. *Liberation Theology: An Evangelical View from the Third World*. London: Marshalls.

Kirk, J. A., 1980. *Theology Encounters Revolution*. Leicester: IVP.

Kirk, J. A., 1986. 'The Middle East Dilemma: A Personal Reflection', *Anvil* 3.3.

Kirk, J. A., 'A Christian Approach to Islam'. Unpublished paper.

Klapp, O., 1969. *The Collective Search for Identity*. New York: Holt, Rinehart & Winston.

Klostermeier, K., 1969. *Hindu and Christian in Vrindaban*. London: SCM Press.

Knitter, P., 1985. *No Other Name?* London: SCM Press.

Kolakowski, L., 1982. *Religion*. London: Collins.

Lamb, C., *The Missionary Theology of Kenneth Cragg*. Unpublished doctoral thesis, University of Birmingham.

Lichtheim, G., 1961. *Marxism*. London: Routledge & Kegan Paul.

Ling, T., 1974. *A History of Religion, East and West*. London: Macmillan.

Luckmann, T., 1970. *The Invisible Religion: The Problem of Religion in Modern Society*. London: Macmillan.

Mangalwadi, V., 1987. *The World of the Gurus*. New Delhi: Nivedit.

Mangalwadi, V., 1989. *Truth and Social Reform*. London: Hodder & Stoughton.

Marmur, D., 1982. *Beyond Survival*. London: Darton, Longman & Todd.

Marx, K., 1972. *The Marx-Engels Reader*, ed. R. Tucker. New York: Norton & Co.

Mathis, T., 1985. *Against John Hick: An Examination of his Philosophy of Religion*. Lanham, MD: University Press of America.

Maududi, A., 1986. *Towards Understanding Islam*. New Delhi.

May, H. F., 1949. *Protestant Churches and Industrial America*. New York: Harper & Bros.

Miguez, J., 1976. *Christians and Marxists: The Mutual Challenge to Revolution*. London: Hodder & Stoughton.

Moore, L., 1971. 'From Profane to Sacred America: Religion and Cultural Revolution in the United States', *Journal of the American Academy of Religion* 39.3.

Moore, S., and B. Myerhoff, eds., 1977. *Secular Ritual*. Amsterdam: Van Gorcum.

Monod, J., 1971. *Chance and Necessity*. London: Collins.

Mulder, D., ed., 1977. *Christians Meeting Muslims*. Geneva: WCC.

Musk, B, 1989. *The Unseen Face of Islam: Sharing the Gospel with Ordinary Muslims*. Eastbourne: Monarch.

Nazir Ali, M., 1983. *Islam: A Christian Perspective*. Exeter: Paternoster Press.

Nazir Ali, M., 1987. *Frontiers in Muslim-Christian Encounter*. Oxford: Regnum Books.

Nazir Ali, M., 'That which is not to be found, but finds us'. Unpublished paper.

Nehru, J., 1989. *The Discovery of India*. Oxford University Press.

Neill, S., 1961. *Christian Faith and Other Faiths: The Christian Dialogue with Other Religions*. London: Oxford University Press.

Netland, H., 1988. 'Exclusivism, Tolerance and Truth', *Evangelical Review of Theololgy* 12.3.

Newbigin, L., 1969. *The Finality of Christ*. London: SCM Press.

Newbigin, L., 1986. *Foolishness to the Greeks*. Geneva: WCC.

Newbigin, L., 1988. 'The Christian Faith and World Religions', in G. Wainwright, ed., *Keeping the Faith: Essays to Mark the Centenary of Lux Mundi*. London: SPCK.

Newbigin, L., 1989. *The Gospel in a Pluralist Culture*. London: SPCK.

Nietzsche, F., 1977. *A Nietzsche Reader*, trans. R. J. Hollingdale. Harmondsworth: Penguin Books.

Pandit, M., 1968. *The Upanishads: Gateways of Knowledge*. India: Ganesh & Co.

Panikkar, R., 1979. *Myth, Faith and Hermeneutics: Cross-Cultural Studies*. New York: Paulist Press.

Parrinder, G., 1987. *Encountering World Religions*. Edinburgh: T. & T. Clark.

Piscatori, J., ed., 1983. *Islam in the Political Process*. Cambridge: Cambridge University Press.

Race, A., 1983. *Christians and Religious Pluralism*. London: SCM Press.

Raj, S., 1986. *The Confusion Called Conversion*. New Delhi.
Richard, L., 1981. *What are They Saying About Christ and the World Religions?* New York: Paulist Press.
Rieff, P., 1979. *Freud: The Mind of the Moralist*. Chicago: Chicago University Press.
Samartha, S., 1971. *Dialogue Between Men of Living Faiths*. Geneva: WCC.
Samartha, S., 1981. *Courage for Dialogue*. Geneva: WCC.
Samuel, V., and C. Sugden, 1983. *The Gospel Among Our Hindu Neighbours*. Bangalore.
Schneider, L., 1970. *Sociological Approach to Religion*. New York: Wiley.
Seddon, P., 1990. *The New Age: An Assessment*. Nottingham: Grove Books.
Segal, R., 1989. *Religion and the Social Sciences*. Missoula, MA: Scholars Press.
Shariati, A., 1979. *On the Sociology of Islam*. Berkeley, CA: Mizan Press.
Shariati, A., 1980. *Marxism and Other Western Fallacies: An Islamic Critique*. Berkeley, CA: Mizan Press.
Sharpe, E., 1975. *Comparative Religion: A History*. London: Duckworth.
Sharpe, E., 1977. *Faith Meets Faith*. London: SCM Press.
Sharpe, E., 1983. *Understanding Religion*. London: Duckworth.
Smart, N., 1983. *Beyond Ideology: Religion and the Future of Western Civilization*. London: Collins.
Snelling, J., 1987. *The Buddhist Handbook: A Complete Guide to Buddhist Teaching and Practice*. London: Century Hutchinson.
Sobrino, J., 1985. *The True Church and the Poor*. London: SCM Press.
Stackhouse, M., 1984. *Creeds, Society and Human Rights: A Study in Three Cultures*. Grand Rapids, MI: Eerdmans.
Stern, J. P., 1978. *Nietzsche*. London: Collins.
Sugden, C., 1985. *Christ's Exclusive Claims and Inter-Faith Dialogue*. Bramcote: Grove Booklets.
Towler, R., 1974. *Homo Religiosus: Sociological Problems in the Study of Religion*. London: Constable.
Troeltsch, E., 1990. *Religion in History*, trans. J. L. Adams and W. E. Bense. Edinburgh: T. & T. Clark.
Vandana, 1978. *Gurus, Ashrams and Christians*. London: Darton, Longman & Todd.

Visser 't Hooft, W., 1963. *No Other Name*. London: SCM Press.
Ward, K., 1986. *The Turn of the Tide: Christian Belief in Britain Today*. London: BBC Publications.
Ward, K., 1987. *Images of Eternity*. London: Darton, Longman & Todd.
Whaling, F., ed., 1985. *The World's Religious Traditions*. Edinburgh: T. & T. Clark.
Whaling, F., ed., 1987. *Religion in Today's World*. Edinburgh: T. & T. Clark.
WCC 1978. *Christian-Muslim Dialogue: Papers from Broumana*. Geneva: WCC.
Wollheim, R., 1971. *Freud*. London: Collins.